Looking for more?? I am constantly adding new volumes of True Crime Case Histories. The series **can be read in any order,** and all books are available in paperback, hardcover, and audiobook.

Check out the complete series on Amazon series at:

https://geni.us/JasonNeal

TRUE CRIME CASE HISTORIES - VOLUME 20

12 DISTURBING TRUE CRIME STORIES

JASON NEAL

JASON NEAL BOOKS

Cover images of:

Sarah Hallow: (top-left)

Ben Fawley: (top-right)

Nathan Matthews: (bottom-left)

Bronwyn Meeks: (bottom-right)

FREE BONUS EBOOK
FOR MY READERS

As my way of saying "Thank you" for reading, I'm giving away a FREE True Crime e-book I think you'll enjoy.

https://TrueCrimeCaseHistories.com

Just visit the link above to let me know where to send your free book!

INTRODUCTION

Some murders reveal something terrifying about human nature: the capacity to plan another person's destruction with cold precision. The cases in this volume aren't crimes of passion or split-second decisions; they're the work of people who had time to think, time to plan, and countless opportunities to stop. Instead, they chose destruction.

A Shot in the Dark – When a ten-year affair finally ended, a respected physician decided that if he couldn't have his mistress, no one could.

Silent Screams – Despite countless welfare checks and reports of suspected abuse, authorities never discovered what was really happening behind closed doors until it was too late.

The House of Secrets – When elderly parents suddenly stopped appearing in public, their daughter had perfectly reasonable explanations for their absence. However, she had been living with a dark secret for years.

The Gilbert Goons – When a popular athlete was brutally attacked at a Halloween party, investigators uncovered a shocking subculture of privileged teenagers who had been terrorizing their community while hiding behind money and influence.

The Hammer Killer – The weapon of choice was always the same, but police couldn't catch the killer who kept systematically destroying families before vanishing without a trace.

The Crown Hill Murder – When a sixteen-year-old girl vanished from her own home, her family had no idea that someone they trusted completely had been planning her death for weeks.

The Facebook Killer – When a controlling husband's threats finally escalated to murder, he decided to document his crime in a way that would shock the world.

The Baseline Killer – Fresh out of prison and free to roam, a predator decided that Phoenix would become his hunting ground for a ten-month reign of terror.

Plus four more disturbing true crime stories.

These weren't crimes committed in moments of rage or desperation. They were carefully orchestrated by people who had decided that other human beings were obstacles to be removed or entertainment to be consumed.

Each story required extensive research through court documents, police interviews, forensic reports, and witness testimony. While I occasionally reconstruct dialogue or protect certain identities, these crimes happened to real people whose final moments were shaped by deliberate cruelty. My goal is to present their stories without sanitization.

Some of these cases took decades to solve, their victims reduced to cold case files until persistence finally provided answers. Others stunned communities that thought they knew their neighbors. A few will make you question whether you can ever really know what someone is capable of.

Many of these cases were suggested by readers who remembered them from their communities or stumbled across forgotten news reports. The most chilling true crime stories are often the ones that didn't make national headlines—the ones that devastated small towns and left families asking how they missed the warning signs.

There are few heroes in these stories, and little hope for true justice or redemption. What you'll find instead is an unflinching look at the depths of human depravity and the ordinary faces that evil can wear.

Additional photos, documents, and case materials can be found at: TrueCrimeCaseHistories.com/volume20

Welcome to the stories nobody wants to believe really happened.

Jason Neal

CHAPTER 1

THE HOUSE OF SECRETS

The knock echoed through the hallway at 12:12 p.m. on September 15, 2023. Detective Superintendent Rob Kirby stood on the front step of 7 Pump Hill in Great Baddow, Essex, studying the modest semi-detached house. Two surveillance cameras stared down at him from above the door like unblinking eyes. Every curtain was drawn tight, sealing the interior from view.

The welfare check should have been routine. An elderly couple's general practitioner hadn't seen them in years. These calls happened constantly, usually ending with embarrassed relatives offering sheepish explanations about forgotten appointments or family miscommunications.

But something felt wrong here. The kind of wrongness that made Kirby's skin crawl.

Inside the house, thirty-five-year-old Virginia McCullough heard the knock and knew her time had come. For four years, three months, and twenty-eight days, she had been waiting for this moment. Living with her secret. Living with what lay hidden behind the walls of this ordinary-looking home.

She walked to the front door in what officers later described as a trance-like state, her footsteps echoing through rooms that held more than furniture and memories.

————

Four years earlier, 7 Pump Hill had been home to what neighbors considered an unremarkable family. Seventy-year-old John McCullough maintained the rigid routine of a man whose life had been built on structure and predictability. Each morning brought the same sequence: medications for his hypertension, type 2 diabetes, and glaucoma, arranged in neat rows on the kitchen counter. Afternoons saw reading sessions in his converted study downstairs. Evening drinks had grown more frequent over the years— Guinness followed by brandy, a pattern as fixed as clockwork.

His wife, Lois, at seventy-one, moved through their home like a woman conducting a symphony of cleanliness. Every surface gleamed under her obsessive attention. She scrubbed floors that were already spotless, organized cupboards that were already perfect. Her agoraphobia had worsened with age, transforming their house into both a sanctuary and a prison. Panic attacks seized her when she ventured too far from familiar walls, so she rarely left.

Their youngest daughter, Virginia, had never found a reason to leave either. At thirty-one, she still occupied the spare bedroom she'd claimed as a teenager, surrounded by art supplies that gathered dust and canvases that remained largely blank. While her four older sisters had married, found careers, and built independent lives, Virginia remained tethered to Pump Hill.

"I'm going to be a successful artist," she told her parents repeatedly. "I'll make a lot of money from my work." The promises came easily, delivered with the confidence of someone who had perfected the art of deception over decades.

To the outside world, the McCulloughs were simply the quiet family who kept to themselves. Neighbors exchanged polite nods with them on the rare occasions they ventured out, but meaningful interactions were few. This invisibility, this careful distance from the community around them, created a cocoon of privacy that would prove tragically convenient.

———

Behind the McCulloughs' front door, Virginia had been orchestrating an elaborate financial fraud that grew more complex with each passing month. She had convinced her parents to give her access to their credit cards, claiming she needed them for household expenses and her art supplies. What they didn't know was that Virginia had been systematically draining their accounts, gambling away thousands of pounds online while purchasing clothes and jewelry for herself.

The lies came naturally to her. When John noticed money missing from their savings account, Virginia produced a forged letter claiming they had been victims of bank fraud. When credit card bills arrived showing purchases they hadn't made, she blamed identity theft and promised to investigate. She even went so far as to stage phone calls, pretending to speak with bank officials about ongoing investigations into the alleged crimes against her parents.

Her siblings had recognized the pattern years earlier. Virginia was a compulsive liar—someone who seemed incapable of telling the truth about even the smallest details of her life. She had spun fantasies about jobs she didn't have, medical conditions she didn't suffer from, and relationships that existed only in her imagination.

By March 2019, the financial house of cards was collapsing. Virginia had accumulated nearly £60,000 in debt using her parents' identities, a sum so massive that no amount of creative accounting could hide it much longer. The monthly bills were becoming impossible to juggle. Soon, inevitably, John and Lois would discover the truth.

The thought terrified Virginia—not because of the pain it would cause her parents, but because of what they might do to her. They could cut off her access to money, throw her out of the house, or report her to the police. She felt trapped, cornered by her own deceptions and with no way out.

It was then that a terrible solution began forming in her mind.

———

Virginia began her preparations in March 2019, moving with the methodical precision of someone planning a business venture rather than a double murder. She started collecting prescription medications from her father's various bottles, taking just a few pills at a time to avoid detection. John's multiple health conditions required an array of powerful drugs, and Virginia calculated that a few missing tablets here and there would go unnoticed.

She researched the medications' effects, studying dosages and potential interactions with the cold efficiency of a pharmacist. By May, she had accumulated what she believed would be a lethal combination of sedatives and other drugs.

But Virginia knew she needed contingency plans. She purchased a sharp kitchen knife from a local store, along with a tool designed to crush pills into powder. She then conducted what she called "guinea pig" tests on her father, slipping small doses of medication into his food and observing the effects. John never noticed the slight changes in his lunch that left him drowsier than usual in the afternoons. He trusted his daughter completely, never questioning the care she provided.

The crushing irony wasn't lost on investigators who later pieced together this timeline: John and Lois McCullough trusted Virginia with their lives, quite literally. They had given her access to their finances, their personal information, and their daily routines. That absolute trust made every aspect of Virginia's planning possible.

———

June 17, 2019, dawned gray and humid—typical early summer weather for Essex. Virginia moved through her morning routine with careful normalcy, preparing breakfast for her parents and discussing mundane household matters. But as evening approached, her pulse quickened with anticipation.

In the kitchen, Virginia began mixing her deadly cocktail. She crushed the accumulated prescription drugs into a fine powder, then stirred the mixture into three alcoholic drinks for her father and one non-alcoholic beverage for her mother. The bitter taste of the medication was masked by the familiar burn of Guinness and brandy that John expected each evening.

Virginia McCullough

John consumed his prepared drinks without hesitation, settling into his chair with the newspaper, as he always did. The powerful sedatives began working immediately, making him drowsy and confused. Lois, who never drank alcohol, took only a small sip of her prepared beverage before setting it aside, complaining about the strange taste.

As the drugs took effect, John became increasingly disoriented. Virginia watched him struggle to focus on his reading, his eyelids growing heavy despite his efforts to stay alert. Eventually, he shuffled off to bed, mumbling about feeling unwell.

Virginia sat awake through the night, listening for any sounds from her parents' bedrooms, her heart pounding as she waited for the poisonous cocktail to complete its work.

———

Virginia crept to her father's bedroom at around 6:00 a.m. on June 18. She found John lying motionless in his bed, his face peaceful in death. The drugs had worked exactly as she had calculated—he had died quietly in his sleep, showing no obvious signs of distress or suffering.

But her relief was short-lived. From the adjoining bedroom came the sound of movement. Lois was still alive.

The smaller dose Virginia's mother had consumed had left her groggy and disoriented but very much breathing. As Virginia stared at her father's still form, a new terror gripped her: Lois would wake up fully, would realize John was dead, and would ask questions Virginia couldn't answer. The discovery of one murder would inevitably unravel everything.

Virginia retrieved the hammer and knife she had hidden in her bedroom weeks earlier. Her hands shook as she gripped the weapons, but her resolve hardened with each step toward her mother's room.

She found Lois in bed, listening to the radio through head-phones as she did every morning—a ritual that had provided comfort during her anxious moments for years. The older woman was vulnerable. Unaware, trusting. She had no reason to fear her own daughter.

Virginia raised the hammer and brought it down on the back of her mother's head with sickening force. The impact jerked

Lois from her drowsy state, tearing the headphones from her ears.

"What are you doing?" Lois cried out, confusion and terror mixing in her voice as she realized her own daughter was attacking her. She tried to roll away, to protect herself, but Virginia struck again.

Blood began pooling on the bedsheets as Lois fought desperately for her life. She raised her hands to ward off the blows, leaving defensive wounds that told the story of her final moments. But Virginia was younger, stronger, and driven by desperation.

When the hammer wasn't enough, Virginia grabbed the knife. She stabbed her mother seven times in the chest and once in the hand as Lois continued to struggle. The violence of the attack left Virginia's own hand cut where the knife slipped during the assault, her blood mixing with her mother's on the bedroom floor.

In those final moments, as Lois's strength ebbed away, Virginia later claimed she held her mother's hand and whispered apologies. Whether this was true or another of her elaborate lies remains known only to Virginia herself.

———

Even as her mother's blood stained the bedroom carpet, Virginia was calculating her next moves. The murders were complete, but now came the equally challenging task of concealing the evidence.

Her first priority was treating her own injury. Within hours of committing double murder, Virginia was sitting calmly in her local general practitioner's office, explaining that she had cut her hand while chopping vegetables for her parents. The doctor cleaned and bandaged the wound without suspicion, noting nothing unusual about the composed young woman's demeanor.

Later that same day, Virginia drove to Chelmsford using her dead father's credit card. She moved through the shops with purpose. She needed sleeping bags, plastic gloves, cleaning supplies, concrete breeze blocks, cement, and sand. The shopping list was practical and efficient. Other customers passed her in the aisles without a second glance, having no idea they were sharing space with someone who had murdered two people just hours earlier.

Returning home, Virginia faced the grisly task of dealing with her parents' bodies. She wrapped each corpse in the newly purchased sleeping bags, struggling with the dead weight as she maneuvered the awkward bundles.

John's body presented the greater challenge. She had to move his remains from the upstairs bedroom to his converted study on the ground floor—a journey that required dragging the wrapped corpse across the landing, down thirteen stairs, and through the narrow hallway. The sleeping bag caught on the stair railings, and Virginia had to stop repeatedly to readjust her grip and catch her breath. The physical exertion left her sweating and exhausted, but she pressed on with determination.

In the study, Virginia began constructing what investigators later called a "makeshift mausoleum." She stacked the concrete breeze blocks around her father's body with the precision of a mason, creating a rectangular tomb that completely enclosed the sleeping bag. She mixed cement to seal the gaps between blocks, working late into the night.

The structure rose from the floor like a bizarre piece of furniture, solid and permanent.

She arranged the study's remaining furniture around the structure, making it appear to be merely an oddly shaped storage unit or decorative feature.

Lois's body received different treatment. Virginia dragged her mother's wrapped remains to the built-in wardrobe in the upstairs bedroom, folding the corpse into the confined space with disturbing efficiency. She sealed the wardrobe doors with electrical tape, winding layer after layer around the handles and frame until no gap remained. For additional security, she stacked several of the heavy concrete blocks in front of the wardrobe, creating a barrier that would deter casual investigation.

The house had become a tomb, but Virginia's work was far from finished. She needed to ensure that no one would come looking for John and Lois, or at least not for a very long time.

————

On the evening of June 18, just hours after murdering her mother, Virginia picked up Lois's mobile phone and composed a text message to one of her sisters:

> Dad and I are at the seaside in Walton this week. Mum x

She followed it with another message that night:

> Good night. Mum x

The messages were the opening moves in an elaborate chess game against reality. Virginia crafted different stories for different people, carefully tailoring each explanation to discourage further inquiry. To relatives, she claimed her parents were on an extended holiday or had permanently relocated to the coast. To medical professionals, she explained that John and Lois were too unwell to attend appointments. To neighbors, she suggested they had moved away to be closer to the sea.

The financial benefits became immediately apparent. Virginia began collecting their state and private pensions payments—money that now flowed directly to her without oversight. She opened new credit accounts in John and Lois's names and contacted her father's pension company, successfully impersonating Lois to ensure continued payments. In at least one documented instance, she mimicked her mother's voice so convincingly during a phone call that her sister believed she was speaking with Lois.

But Virginia's gambling addiction consumed the stolen funds as quickly as she acquired them. Over the following months, she lost over £21,000 on online betting sites, chasing impossible jackpots while her parents' life savings evaporated into digital slot machines and sports wagers. By the end of her four-year deception, she had fraudulently obtained nearly £150,000 and squandered most of it.

———

Perhaps the most disturbing aspect of Virginia's crime wasn't the murders themselves, but what came after. She continued living in the house on Pump Hill as if nothing had happened, going about her daily routines while her parents' bodies decomposed just feet away.

The practical challenges were significant. Virginia burned scented candles constantly and used air fresheners throughout the house, creating a sickening sweetness that masked the more sinister smells. Her careful sealing and wrapping of the bodies had helped contain the worst of the decomposition odors.

Virginia also became a fixture in the neighborhood during this period, though her behavior grew increasingly eccentric. She began appearing at Russell Thornton's door across the street almost daily, leaving strange notes when he didn't answer. The messages offered to draw his dog's portrait for free or rambled about her "seriously ill" relatives—a darkly ironic reference to the corpses in her home.

She left bizarre gifts for neighbors: LED lights, Christmas decorations, fresh food, even old sandals and anti-wrinkle cream. The presents seemed random but weren't threatening enough to cause serious alarm. To recipients, Virginia appeared lonely and slightly odd rather than dangerous.

Russell began keeping a logbook of these encounters after Virginia's visits became obsessive. She would knock on his door multiple times per day, sometimes leaving elaborate notes filled with personal details. The attention was unwanted but seemed harmless—the actions of an isolated woman seeking human connection while living alongside the dead.

———

In March 2020, the COVID-19 pandemic reached Britain, bringing lockdowns and social distancing measures that inadvertently provided Virginia with the perfect cover for her parents' continued absence. Suddenly, it was not only reasonable but expected that elderly, vulnerable people would avoid contact with family and friends.

Virginia exploited these restrictions brilliantly. When relatives called asking to visit, she explained that John and Lois were isolating due to health concerns. When medical appointments were cancelled, she blamed pandemic fears. The virus had given her an unassailable excuse for her parents' invisibility.

She installed two surveillance cameras above her front door, monitoring who approached the house. The curtains remained permanently drawn, sealing the interior from curious eyes. Her earlier stories about her parents' seaside retirement now seemed prescient—of course they would stay away during a dangerous pandemic.

As restrictions eased in 2021 and 2022, Virginia had to evolve her methods. She arranged for printed greeting cards and gifts to be delivered in her parents' names for birthdays and holidays, maintaining the illusion that John and Lois remained thoughtful and engaged with their family.

By 2023, however, Virginia was making increasingly desperate attempts to maintain her facade. She began calling the police to report minor neighborhood issues—noisy neighbors and suspicious people lurking nearby. In one particularly audacious move, she even claimed to have been assaulted, bringing an officer to investigate at the very house where her parents' bodies lay concealed. The officer found nothing suspicious, though he noted Virginia's slightly odd demeanor.

The same elaborate lies that had fooled family and friends for years were beginning to feel rehearsed. Hollow. Still,

Virginia pressed on, trapped now not just by her original crimes but by the weight of the deception itself.

———

Dr. James Morrison had been John McCullough's general practitioner for over a decade. He knew his elderly patient's medical history intimately: the diabetes that required careful monitoring, the glaucoma that threatened his sight, the various medications that needed regular adjustment.

What troubled Dr. Morrison was the complete absence of contact. John had missed dozens of appointments over the past few years, failed to collect prescription medications that were essential for his health conditions, and couldn't be reached directly despite his serious medical needs.

Each time the doctor's office called, Virginia provided explanations. Her parents were traveling, they were unwell, they were staying elsewhere. But the pattern of persistent cancellations and excuses had become impossible to ignore. No responsible doctor could allow elderly patients with serious health conditions to remain without medical supervision for so long.

In early September 2023, Dr. Morrison made a decision that would finally unravel Virginia's carefully constructed lies. Citing his duty of care, he contacted Essex County Council's safeguarding team to report his concerns about John and Lois McCullough's welfare.

The safeguarding team immediately contacted Essex Police on September 13, requesting a welfare check on the elderly couple. Officers initially treated it as a routine missing persons inquiry, reaching out to Virginia as the known resident of the household.

Virginia's response was characteristically elaborate. She claimed her parents were traveling abroad and due to return in October 2023. She provided detailed but unverifiable accounts of their supposed travels, weaving the same kind of intricate lies she had perfected over four years.

However, Detective Superintendent Rob Kirby wasn't satisfied. The detailed excuses without any way to directly contact John or Lois not only felt rehearsed but seemed too convenient. Something about Virginia's responses triggered his investigative instincts.

———

Two days later, on September 15, Essex Police had escalated the case from a missing persons inquiry to a potential murder investigation. Armed with a search warrant, Kirby and his team arrived at 7 Pump Hill just after noon.

The house felt wrong from the moment they approached. The surveillance cameras, the drawn curtains, the oppressive silence—everything suggested secrets hidden behind ordinary walls.

When they knocked, Virginia answered in what officers later described as a trance-like state. However, confronted by the police presence in her home, her long-held secret unraveled in an instant.

"I did know that this day would come eventually," Virginia said, her voice remarkably calm as body-worn cameras captured every word. "I deserve to get what's coming."

She confessed immediately, directing officers to the locations where she had hidden her parents' bodies. Her demeanor was eerily composed, matter-of-fact—as if she were providing directions to a lost tourist rather than admitting to double murder.

"Cheer up, at least you've caught the bad guy," she told the stunned officers, her dark humor intact even in the face of life imprisonment.

———

Officers found exactly what Virginia had described, though the reality was far worse than investigators had imagined. In John's former study, concealed within the makeshift mausoleum Virginia had constructed, lay the mummified remains of the retired lecturer. The structure was expertly built and sealed with concrete blocks and cement.

The sight that greeted officers was beyond their experience. Virginia had essentially turned her father's study into a tomb disguised as furniture. Blankets draped the rectangular enclosure while her grandfather's paintings hung on the exposed surfaces. Books and papers were arranged nearby to suggest the room remained in normal use—a grotesque charade that had hidden its grim contents for years.

Upstairs, sealed in the wardrobe with multiple layers of electrical tape, officers discovered Lois's skeletal remains still wrapped in the sleeping bag Virginia had purchased the day after the murder. The advanced state of decomposition told its own story—these bodies had been here for years, slowly decaying while their daughter lived her life around them.

Virginia cooperated fully with the investigation, providing passwords to her devices and directing officers to evidence they might have missed. When asked about the murder weapons, she responded with chilling precision: "The hammer will still have blood on it. It's rusted but will still have traces on it."

―――――

The evidence was overwhelming. Virginia's calm confessions, the physical evidence, the elaborate four-year deception—it all painted a picture of calculated murder followed by methodical concealment.

As investigators pieced together the full scope of her crimes, the psychological aspects became almost as disturbing as the murders themselves. Virginia had been diagnosed with autism spectrum disorder and paranoia, conditions her defense team argued provided some explanation for her actions. Her rigid thinking may have led her to see murder as the only solution to her financial problems.

But Mr. Justice Johnson rejected these explanations when Virginia appeared for sentencing. While acknowledging her mental health conditions, he found that she was fully responsible for her actions, understanding right from wrong throughout the planning and execution of her crimes.

When Virginia McCullough pleaded guilty to both counts of murder on July 4, 2024, she spared her surviving family the trauma of a trial. On October 11, Justice Johnson sentenced her to life imprisonment with a minimum term of thirty-six years.

"Your parents were entitled to feel safe in their own beds and their own home," the judge told her, "and they were entitled to feel safe with their daughter. You made a full, conscious, and deliberate decision to murder each of your parents."

Virginia showed no emotion as the sentence was delivered. She will be eligible for parole on October 3, 2059, at age seventy-one—the same age her mother had been when Virginia murdered her.

————

The surviving McCullough family issued a statement describing their devastation at the cruel deaths of their parents. They remembered John as a caring, hardworking man with a passion for education and a great sense of humor. Lois was recalled as kind and thoughtful, a devoted mother and grandmother who maintained friendships around the world despite her agoraphobia.

Detective Superintendent Rob Kirby, who had led the investigation, struggled to find words for what his team had discovered. "The details of this case shock and horrify even the most experienced of murder detectives," he said, describing Virginia as "an intelligent manipulator who chose to kill her parents callously, without a thought for them or those who continue to suffer as a result of their loss."

The house on Pump Hill stands empty now, its windows still covered, its surveillance cameras dark. Neighbors who once received Virginia's strange gifts and rambling notes now understand the terrible secret that lay behind those drawn curtains.

For four years, three months, and twenty-eight days, Virginia McCullough had hidden in plain sight, living with decomposing bodies while maintaining an elaborate fiction that fooled family, friends, and authorities. Her crime was not just murder but a sustained violation of the most basic human bonds—the trust between parent and child, the sanctity of family, and the assumption that love provides protection rather than danger.

CHAPTER 2

THE HAMMER KILLER

The screaming started at 3:47 a.m.

Kimberly Haubenschild jolted awake to a flash of white-hot pain across her skull. In the darkness of her Aurora bedroom, she could make out a silhouette of someone standing over her bed, arm raised, something heavy clutched in their fist. Before she could fully process what was happening, the figure brought the object down again with tremendous force.

The sound startled the intruder as much as it did Kimberly. The dark figure froze for just a moment, then turned and fled. James bolted upright beside her, instantly alert from his wife's terrified scream. Blood streaming down her face, Kimberly gasped out what had happened as James took in the chaos of their bedroom and his wife's battered head. Without hesitation, he leaped from the bed and chased after the attacker.

Despite suffering skull fractures that would require extensive medical treatment, James chased the intruder through their house and out into the frigid Colorado morning. However, the figure had vanished into the pre-dawn darkness, leaving behind only the metallic taste of terror and a ransacked purse near their home.

As paramedics treated Kimberly's injuries and police processed the scene, no one could have imagined that this was just the beginning.

———

Five days later, on January 9, 1984, Donna Dixon was coming home from another long shift. At twenty-eight, she had built a successful career as a flight attendant, traveling the country but always returning to her quiet Aurora neighborhood. The garage door rumbled open as she pulled into her driveway that evening, the familiar sound of home after days in sterile airport terminals and cramped airplane cabins.

She was gathering her purse and overnight bag when she heard footsteps behind her. Donna turned, expecting to see a neighbor, but instead found herself face-to-face with a stranger. Before she could speak, something heavy crashed into her skull with devastating force, and her world exploded into darkness.

When her boyfriend arrived hours later, he found Donna unconscious on the garage floor, blood pooling around her head. Her car door hung open, her belongings scattered. A hammer lay nearby, its surface stained dark red. The attack had been so vicious that Donna slipped into a coma, her brain struggling to function after the trauma.

In the hospital, doctors worked frantically to save her life. The beating had caused severe brain damage, and for days, no one knew if she would survive. When Donna finally regained consciousness weeks later, she had to relearn basic functions—how to walk, how to speak, even how to remember. The physical evidence told a story she couldn't recall: She had been brutally raped on the concrete floor of her own garage.

Aurora police processed both crime scenes but found no clear connections beyond the use of a hammer. Random home invasions weren't unheard of, though the level of violence was disturbing. They interviewed neighbors, checked on known offenders, and followed up on tips. Unfortunately, with no witnesses and limited forensic technology in 1984, leads were scarce.

The attacks had been motiveless and savage. Nothing valuable had been stolen from either home. The perpetrator seemed driven by something far darker than simple theft.

———

Patricia Smith was folding laundry in her Lakewood home when death walked through her door.

At fifty, Patricia had recently started her own interior decorating business and was helping care for her grandchildren following her daughter's divorce. January 10, 1984, was supposed to be a quiet afternoon. She planned to pick up her granddaughter from school at 3:00 p.m., then spend the evening with the children.

But when 3:00 p.m. came and went with no sign of their grandmother, Patricia's grandchildren and a cousin grew worried. They walked the few blocks home, expecting to find her car in the driveway. Instead, they found the front door unlocked.

The children called out as they entered the house, their voices echoing in the unusual silence. When they reached the family room, they stopped in horror.

Patricia lay on the floor, positioned on top of a neatly folded Winnie-the-Pooh blanket. Her arms were crossed over her chest as if she were lying in a casket. Blood stained the carpet around her head, and her clothing had been pulled down to her ankles. Seventeen crushing hammer blows had ended her life.

A bloodied hammer sat beside her body like a calling card.

The children ran to neighbors, who immediately called the police. Lakewood detectives arrived to find one of the most disturbing crime scenes they had ever encountered. Patricia had clearly been sexually assaulted before being bludgeoned to death, but the positioning of her body suggested something even more sinister. The killer had taken time to pose her, to humiliate her even in death.

Like the Aurora cases, expensive items remained untouched throughout the house. Patricia's purse had been rifled through, its contents scattered, but cash and jewelry lay undisturbed. The killer hadn't come for money.

———

Six days later, Connie Bennett couldn't reach her son by phone.

Bruce and Debra Bennett, both in their twenties, had recently moved into a new home on East Center Drive in Aurora with their two daughters—seven-year-old Melissa and three-year-old Vanessa. The young family worked together at a furniture store that Connie also helped manage, and when Bruce and Debra failed to show up for work on January 16, she knew something was wrong.

Connie drove to their house and knocked on the front door. No answer. She tried the handle and found it unlocked.

"Bruce? Debra?" she called out as she stepped inside.

The silence felt wrong. Heavy. Then she saw the blood.

At the foot of the stairs, her son Bruce lay motionless, his throat slashed, his head battered beyond recognition. Blood soaked into the carpet around him, evidence of a fierce struggle that had ranged throughout the house.

Connie's legs nearly gave out as she climbed the stairs, following the trail of violence. In the master bedroom, she found Debra's body. The young mother had been beaten so savagely that her face was unrecognizable. Her nightgown was torn, pushed up around her waist.

But the true horror awaited in the children's room.

Seven-year-old Melissa lay in her bed, her small body broken and still. Like her mother and Patricia Smith, she had been sexually assaulted before being murdered with crushing blows to her head.

Between the bed and wall, Connie found three-year-old Vanessa—barely alive, gasping for breath through a shattered jaw and skull. Pieces of bone clogged her airway, and her tiny limbs were bent at unnatural angles. The killer had bludgeoned this toddler with the same fury he had shown her family, then left her to die.

Connie's screams brought neighbors running, and within minutes, Aurora police and paramedics swarmed the scene. As Vanessa was rushed to the hospital, detectives tried to process what they were seeing. The weapon was obvious—a claw hammer left behind like a signature—but the sheer brutality defied explanation.

This wasn't just murder. It was annihilation.

———

Detective units from Aurora and Lakewood began comparing notes as the similarities became impossible to ignore. Four separate attacks in twelve days. All involved hammer assaults. All included sexual violence against female victims. All occurred during nighttime home invasions where nothing of value was stolen.

The killer entered through open garage doors or unlocked entrances, suggesting he prowled neighborhoods looking for opportunities. Once inside, he unleashed devastating violence with whatever blunt instrument he could find— though hammers seemed to be his weapon of choice.

Most disturbing was the escalation. The January 4 attacks had left survivors. Patricia Smith's murder on January 10 marked the first fatality. Then came the wholesale slaughter of the Bennett family, including small children.

Police realized they were hunting a serial killer unlike any they had encountered. The randomness of his targets made him nearly impossible to track. The violence of his attacks suggested deep psychological damage. And somewhere in the Denver metropolitan area, he was still free.

Community meetings were held. Residents installed new locks and security systems, and parents checked on their children obsessively. However, as days turned to weeks with no new attacks, investigators began to wonder if their killer had moved on—or if he was simply lying dormant, waiting for his next opportunity to strike.

———

Then, nothing. No more hammer attacks. No more home invasions. No more broken families. The violence that had terrorized the Denver area for twelve horrific days simply stopped, as suddenly and mysteriously as it had begun.

Detectives weren't sure what to make of the silence. Had the killer been spooked by the increased police presence? Had he left the area? Was he planning something even worse? The uncertainty was almost as terrifying as the attacks themselves.

Days became weeks and weeks became months, but there was no sign of the hammer killer.

———

Years passed, then decades. The hammer murder cases remained open, but with no viable leads. Detectives interviewed hundreds of potential suspects, processed evidence using the best technology available in the 1980s, and followed up on thousands of tips from the public. Tragically, nothing yielded results, and the cases went cold.

For the survivors, the silence brought no peace. Kimberly Haubenschild, now Rice, suffered from PTSD and migraines, constantly checking her locks and advising neighbors to do the same. She couldn't shake the image of that dark silhouette standing over her bed, couldn't forget the sound of the hammer cutting through the air.

Donna Dixon recovered from her brain injuries through sheer determination, relearning how to walk and speak. She eventually married Ron Holm, who had stood by her throughout the grueling rehabilitation, but the trauma lived in her body. There were phantom pains, sudden anxiety attacks, and the feeling that safety was always just an illusion.

Vanessa Bennett faced the most difficult journey of all. The three-year-old who had survived the massacre grew up without any real memory of her family. Countless surgeries repaired her shattered bones, but nothing could fix the psychological damage. She struggled with depression, PTSD, and eventually drug addiction as she tried to cope with trauma she barely remembered but could never escape.

By the 1990s, the families had lost hope of ever learning who had destroyed their lives. The hammer killer had vanished, leaving behind only scars and unanswered questions.

———

In February 2001, Kevin Humphreys was reviewing old evidence with new technology. The retired Colorado Bureau of Investigation analyst had seen DNA revolutionize criminal investigations, and he wondered if the hammer murder cases might finally yield their secrets.

He extracted DNA from carpeting and a comforter found in Melissa Bennett's bedroom—biological material left behind during the sexual assault. The profile showed an unknown male. Humphreys entered it into CODIS, the FBI's national database, but he found no matches.

Around the same time, forensic biologist Cynthia Kramer was analyzing evidence from Patricia Smith's murder scene.

DNA extracted from carpeting where her body was found produced a profile that made her pulse quicken.

It matched the unknown male from the Bennett case perfectly.

After seventeen years, investigators finally had proof that the same man who had killed Patricia Smith had also killed the Bennett family. Of course, knowing the cases were connected didn't identify the killer. The DNA profile sat in the database for another sixteen years, a genetic fingerprint without a name, waiting for a match that might never come.

The probability of these profiles matching by coincidence was virtually impossible—just one chance in 13 nonillion. That's a 13 followed by 31 zeros.

———

On a routine day in July 2018, a computer match would finally shatter the mystery that had haunted Colorado for thirty-four years.

Nevada prison officials were entering inmate DNA profiles into the CODIS database as part of standard processing. When they uploaded the profile for one particular inmate, a fifty-seven-year-old man who had been locked away since the 1980s, the computer immediately flagged a match.

The profile belonged to Alex Christopher Ewing, a Nevada Department of Corrections inmate serving time for attempted murder and assault. His DNA matched the genetic evidence from both the Bennett family murders and Patricia Smith's death.

Alex Christopher Ewing

The notification sent shockwaves through law enforcement agencies in both states. For more than three decades, the man responsible for terrorizing the Denver area had been sitting in a Nevada prison cell, unknown to Colorado investigators as their most wanted suspect.

But who was Alex Christopher Ewing? And how had he managed to evade justice for so long while locked away in plain sight?

———

Alex Christopher Ewing was born in 1960, making him just twenty-three years old during his Colorado killing spree. Little is known about his early life or what drove him to such extreme violence. Court records and prison files offer few insights into his psychology or motivations.

What investigators did uncover was the chilling timeline of his crimes—and the reason the Colorado attacks had stopped so abruptly.

After the Bennett family murders on January 16, 1984, Ewing had indeed fled the state. Rather than disappearing into anonymity, however, he had continued his pattern of brutal violence across the Southwest, leaving a trail of battered victims in his wake.

———

Eleven days after murdering the Bennett family, Ewing was prowling the quiet streets of Kingman, Arizona. Roy Williams was sleeping peacefully in his home when he was jolted awake by something crashing into his skull with tremendous force.

Ewing had picked up a twenty-five-pound slab of granite rock and hurled it at the sleeping man's head. The impact caused severe head trauma and opened a massive gash that would require extensive stitches to close. Blood poured from the wound as Williams struggled to understand what was happening.

The attack bore all the hallmarks of Ewing's Colorado crimes—a random nighttime assault on a sleeping victim using a heavy blunt object. Williams had never seen his attacker before and had nothing of value worth stealing. Like the hammer murders, this seemed driven by pure sadistic pleasure.

But this time, Ewing had made a mistake. His footprints in the dirt outside Williams's home were clear and distinctive. When police arrived, they took careful measurements and began searching the area for anyone whose shoes might match.

Two days later, they found Alex Ewing. His shoe prints matched the prints perfectly, and he had no alibi for the night of the attack. The twenty-four-year-old drifter was arrested and charged with attempted murder and burglary.

Due to jail overcrowding in Mojave County, Ewing was transferred to a facility in Utah to await trial. For the first time since his killing spree began, he was behind bars—but his violent impulses weren't finished yet.

———

In August 1984, Ewing was being transported from the Utah jail back to Arizona for his court hearing. The Mojave County Sheriff's Department was moving him in a prison van when they stopped at a gas station in Henderson, Nevada.

Ewing saw his chance, and he took it. He broke free from his restraints and bolted from the van, leaving his guards scrambling to pursue him. Running through the parking lot in his orange jumpsuit, Ewing ducked into a nearby K-Mart store. In the chaos of aisles and shoppers, he managed to steal a pair of shorts and change out of his prison clothes.

Now dressed like any other customer, he slipped out of the store and into the suburban streets of Henderson. Night was falling, and Ewing began prowling the residential neighborhoods just as he had in Colorado and Arizona. His escape had lasted only hours, but that was enough time for one final act of violence.

———

Christopher and Nancy Barry were sleeping in their Henderson home with their young children when Ewing broke in through their garage. The layout was familiar—an open entrance, a quiet suburban house, and sleeping victims unaware of the danger creeping toward them.

In the garage, Ewing found an ax handle. He gripped the wooden weapon and made his way toward the master bedroom, following the same ritual he had perfected in Colorado. But Christopher and Nancy Berry were not easy targets.

When Ewing began his attack, both adults fought back with desperate fury. They knew their children were sleeping nearby; they had to survive to protect them. The garage and bedroom became a battlefield as the couple struggled against their attacker.

Ewing brought the ax handle down again and again, battering Christopher's head and face. Nancy tried to shield her husband and received multiple fractures to her hands as she blocked the blows. Christopher's jaw was shattered and knocked out of alignment. The beating damaged his eye socket and destroyed his sense of smell.

But they refused to give up. Their resistance and the sounds of struggle may have prevented Ewing from escalating to murder, as he had in Colorado. Or perhaps the knowledge that he was an escaped prisoner being actively hunted made him more cautious about spending time at the scene.

Whatever the reason, Ewing fled the Barry home before finishing what he had started. Christopher and Nancy survived, though both would carry permanent injuries from the attack. Their children slept through the entire assault, never knowing how close they had come to waking up orphaned.

———

Two days after his escape, Alex Ewing was located by National Park Service rangers near Lake Mead and taken into custody without incident. The violent young man who had terrorized families across three states was finally in chains.

On March 1, 1985, Ewing was sentenced to an eight-to-forty-year term for the assault on the Barrys, enhanced by deadly weapon charges to an effective total of 110 years in the Nevada prison system.

At just twenty-four years old, Alex Christopher Ewing disappeared behind bars. He would remain there for the next thirty-four years, aging from a violent young predator into an elderly inmate, while the families he had destroyed in Colorado continued searching for answers that sat locked away in a Nevada prison cell.

———

Even after his identity was revealed, the fundamental question remained: Why had Alex Ewing committed such horrific crimes?

Court records, psychological evaluations, and prison files offer few insights into his motivations. He never confessed to the Colorado murders, never expressed remorse for his victims, and never explained what drove him to such extreme violence.

What investigators could piece together was a behavioral pattern that suggested a particular type of predator. Ewing seemed to derive satisfaction from absolute domination and control. His victims ranged from elderly women to toddlers, suggesting his violence wasn't driven by sexual preference but by a desire to inflict maximum trauma on the most vulnerable people he could find.

The fact that he targeted complete strangers also indicated this wasn't personal vengeance or robbery gone wrong. Ewing appeared to select victims based on opportunity and vulnerability rather than any connection to his own life. He was a predator in the purest sense—hunting for the simple pleasure of causing pain.

The escalation from assault to murder to family annihilation suggested an increasing tolerance for violence, as if each attack required more brutality to satisfy whatever psychological need drove him. By the time he reached the Bennett family, Ewing had progressed to killing children as young as seven and attempting to murder a three-year-old.

His lack of emotion during and after his crimes was disturbing. Witnesses who encountered Ewing during his arrests noted his apparent indifference to the suffering he had caused. Police officers who processed him described a young man who seemed completely detached from the horror he had inflicted.

Without a confession or detailed psychological evaluation, the full answer to "why" may never be known. What is clear is that Alex Christopher Ewing represented one of the most dangerous types of criminal—a predator driven by internal compulsions to hurt innocent people, with no apparent conscience to restrain his actions.

———

When Colorado authorities finally identified their decades-old suspect in 2018, Ewing fought extradition with the same determination he had once used to evade capture. For eighteen months, he filed appeals and legal challenges, trying to avoid facing murder charges for crimes he had committed thirty-four years earlier.

But in February 2020, the Nevada Supreme Court denied his final appeal. At sixty years old, gray-haired and wearing glasses, Alex Christopher Ewing was finally transported to Colorado to face justice for the hammer murders.

The trials began in 2021, bringing together evidence that had been carefully preserved for nearly four decades. Prosecutors presented the DNA matches, crime scene photographs, and testimony from surviving family members who had waited their entire adult lives for this moment.

Vanessa Bennett, now forty-one, faced her family's killer in court. The three-year-old who had nearly died from his savage assault had grown into a woman despite the odds. She spoke of permanent physical damage—her jaw and ankles still bore the effects of his attack. More devastating were the psychological scars: PTSD, depression, and struggles with addiction as she tried to cope with trauma she barely remembered but could never escape.

"I didn't just lose my parents and my sister," she told Ewing during his sentencing. "I lost the person who I was supposed to be. There's no fixing what he took from me."

Even as evidence mounted against him, Ewing maintained his innocence, claiming the proceedings were "rigged" and that prosecutors just wanted "the conviction" rather than the truth. His defiance rang hollow against the weight of genetic evidence and decades of investigative work.

On August 6, 2021, a jury found Alex Ewing guilty of murdering Bruce, Debra, and Melissa Bennett. The judge sentenced him to three consecutive life terms. A separate trial for Patricia Smith's murder followed in 2022, resulting in another life sentence.

————

Today, Alex Christopher Ewing sits in the Colorado Territorial Correctional Facility in Cañon City, serving four consecutive life sentences. At sixty-two, he will never see freedom again.

CHAPTER 3
SILENT SCREAMS

The 911 call came in at 3:43 p.m. on a sweltering Thursday afternoon in August 2020. Sarah Hallow's voice crackled through the dispatcher's headset, frantic and breathless.

"I need an ambulance! My stepdaughter—she's not breathing!"

Within minutes, Elk River police officers and paramedics raced through the tree-lined streets toward The Depot at Elk River Station apartment complex. The sprawling development sat just off Highway 10, its brick facades and manicured lawns giving no hint of the horror waiting inside the apartment.

Officer Martinez was first through the door. Brett Hallow, a stocky man in his early thirties, met him at the entrance with hollow eyes and directed him toward a back bedroom. The scene that greeted Martinez would haunt him for years.

On the carpeted floor lay a tiny girl, her body so frail that her ribs showed through pale skin. Sarah Hallow knelt beside her, performing chest compressions, but something felt wrong immediately. The child's skin was dry—unusual for someone pulled from a bathtub. Her fingertips had turned blue, and when Martinez knelt closer, he noticed the telltale stiffness of rigor mortis beginning to set in.

This wasn't a drowning victim. This was a child who had been dead for hours.

———

Eight years earlier, Autumn Lee Hallow entered the world six weeks early in a Coon Rapids hospital. Despite the premature birth, she was a fighter from the start. Her mother, Kelsey Kruse, was young but devoted, and her father, Brett, seemed eager to embrace parenthood.

Autumn grew into a vibrant little girl with an infectious smile and boundless creativity. She loved to draw elaborate pictures, dance to music only she could hear, and practice gymnastics moves in the living room. Her teachers at Lincoln Elementary School described her as kind and helpful, always the first to volunteer when someone needed assistance.

But like many modern families, the Hallows' story was complicated. Brett and Kelsey's relationship didn't survive, and by the time Autumn was old enough to understand, her parents shared custody through a court-ordered arrangement. Fifty-fifty time with each parent, a perfectly normal situation for thousands of divorced couples across the country.

When Brett met Sarah Nasby, it seemed like a fresh start. Sarah had her own daughter from a previous relationship, and together, they created what looked like a typical blended family. Brett and Sarah married, and suddenly, Autumn had not just a stepmother but a stepsister too.

To outsiders, everything appeared fine. The family lived in a decent apartment complex, the children were enrolled in school, and neighbors occasionally saw them coming and going like any other busy household.

But neighbors also heard other things.

———

Sabrina McWilliam lived close enough to the Hallows that sound traveled easily between their units. She first noticed the yelling sometime in 2019—loud, angry voices that seemed directed at children. At first, she dismissed it. Every parent lost their temper occasionally, and apartment living meant overhearing your neighbors' worst moments.

But the incidents kept happening. And getting worse.

The voices weren't just stern parental corrections. They were prolonged episodes of screaming, cursing, and what sounded like genuine terror from small children. Sometimes McWilliam could hear a child crying desperately, other times the sound of what might have been physical struggling.

On multiple occasions throughout 2019 and into 2020, she picked up her phone and dialed 911. Each time, she carefully explained to dispatchers that something didn't sound right next door. Each time, officers responded and knocked on the Hallows' door. And each time, they left without taking any action.

The pattern became grimly predictable. McWilliam heard disturbing sounds—children screaming, adults yelling threats, and sometimes what sounded like impacts against walls. She would call the police. Officers would arrive, speak briefly with Brett and Sarah, and conclude that everything was fine.

Other neighbors began calling, too. Anonymous reports filtered in regularly about loud juvenile crying, sounds of children being hit, and verbal abuse that could be heard through the walls. Between 2018 and August 2020, Elk River Police responded to the Hallows' apartment thirty-one times.

But the children always appeared fine when officers arrived. Brett and Sarah had explanations for everything—a sick child, video game excitement, and normal family disagreements. The officers documented their visits and moved on to other calls.

What none of them realized was that just beyond their sight, a nightmare was unfolding in slow motion.

———

While neighbors wondered about the screaming, Kelsey Kruse was fighting her own battle. Throughout 2019, her son—Autumn's older brother—had begun returning from visits to his father's house with disturbing injuries. Bruises covered his small body from forehead to feet. When Kelsey rushed him to the emergency room, doctors were concerned enough to file a report with child protective services.

An Elk River detective investigated but concluded they were "unable to substantiate any sort of abuse allegations." The case was closed.

Kelsey's anxiety deepened when she attempted to get an Order for Protection against Sarah in 2017, detailing how her son came home with unexplained bruises. The court denied the petition, ruling that it failed to show "immediate and present danger." A child protection assessment was opened but later closed for lack of evidence.

By late 2019, Kelsey made a heartbreaking decision. She stopped allowing her son to visit Brett and Sarah's apartment; the risk was too great. However, Autumn continued her regular visits, spending alternating weeks with each parent as the custody agreement required.

Then came 2020, and everything changed.

———

When the COVID-19 pandemic hit Minnesota in March, Brett suddenly had a new excuse. He began refusing to return Autumn to her mother, claiming safety concerns about virus exposure. What had been a regular custody exchange became a protracted standoff.

Kelsey hadn't seen her daughter since January 26, 2020. She called police repeatedly, explaining that Brett was violating their court order and that she feared for Autumn's safety. Each time, officers told her it was a civil custody matter. When she begged for welfare checks, they would drive to the apartment complex and accept Brett's assurances that everything was fine.

On June 21, 2020, officers finally conducted a visual confirmation of Autumn's well-being. Instead of allowing them inside for a proper check, Brett simply had the eight-year-old wave to them from the apartment balcony.

That glimpse from a distance was the last time any official would see Autumn alive.

———

What Kelsey couldn't know—what no one outside that apartment could fully comprehend—was the systematic torture taking place just yards from where officers stood during their welfare checks.

Inside the apartment, Autumn's life had become a waking nightmare. Brett and Sarah had developed an elaborate system of punishments that went far beyond any reasonable definition of discipline. When Autumn wet herself—something common for stressed children—she would be tied up with a brown leather belt. When she tried to sneak food because she was hungry, she would be wrapped so tightly in a red sleeping bag that only her head remained exposed.

Sometimes they would tie her hands behind her back with a long shirt, then leave her bound overnight. She would sleep restrained on the living room floor, in the kitchen, or sometimes in the bathtub itself—wherever her captors decided she deserved to spend the night.

The "infractions" that triggered these punishments were the desperate actions of a child under extreme duress. Autumn wet herself because she was terrified. She tried to sneak food because she was being systematically starved. Her body was crying out for basic human needs, but Brett and Sarah interpreted every natural response as defiance requiring escalated punishment.

Food became a weapon of control. They withheld meals for extended periods, watching as Autumn's small frame grew smaller. By August 2020, the eight-year-old weighed just thirty-three pounds—roughly the same as what she had weighed at age four.

The apartment's surveillance cameras, originally installed for security, captured hours of this abuse. Video evidence would later show Brett and Sarah beating, starving, and restraining Autumn throughout 2019 and into 2020. They had created their own documentary of torture, never imagining anyone would see it.

———

By early August 2020, Autumn was barely recognizable as the vibrant child she had once been. Her hair was falling out in patches from malnutrition. Her muscles had atrophied from starvation. She was essentially confined to the bathroom, imprisoned in the place where her life would ultimately end.

The exact sequence of events on August 13 would later be reconstructed through witness statements and physical evidence. That morning, both Brett and Sarah were in the bathroom with Autumn. Her six-year-old brother heard her screaming, followed by a loud bang that suggested someone had been slammed against a wall or fixture.

Autumn told her father she would rather die than clean up vomit—a statement that would prove tragically prophetic. Brett grabbed her by the shoulder and neck area. Sarah then grabbed the child by the throat and pressed her against the wall for ten seconds. The stepmother struck Autumn hard enough to cause substantial bodily harm.

Hours later, Brett woke from a nap at around 3:00 p.m. and heard a thud from the bathroom. He found Sarah yelling at Autumn while pouring hot water on her motionless body. The child was already beyond help.

Instead of immediately calling for emergency assistance, they moved Autumn's body and began staging the scene. When Sarah finally dialed 911 at 3:43 p.m., she had her story ready: Autumn had been taking a shower unsupervised and somehow drowned in a few inches of water.

———

Paramedics had seen drowning victims before, and something about this scene felt wrong from the moment they entered the bedroom. Autumn's body showed none of the typical signs of water immersion. Her skin was dry, her hair only slightly damp. The stiffness in her limbs suggested she had been dead for hours, not the forty minutes Sarah claimed.

Detective Williams arrived shortly after the paramedics pronounced Autumn dead. He began walking through the apartment, noting details that didn't align with the drowning story. There was blood in the bathroom—not just traces, but enough that crime scene technicians would later use luminol to reveal extensive spatter patterns in the shower area.

Autumn's body told its own story. Paired puncture wounds marked her forehead, as if something pronged had been pressed into her skin. Bruises covered her hands, arms, and hips. Her emaciated condition was immediately obvious— this was a child who had been systematically starved.

Williams noticed something else: Sarah had a fresh scratch running from her forehead, down to her nose, and across her cheek. It looked like the kind of mark a desperate child might leave while fighting for her life.

When officers separated Brett and Sarah for questioning, both stuck to the drowning story. They claimed they had found Autumn face down in the bathtub. They had pulled her out and attempted CPR, and it was all just a terrible accident.

But investigators had already seen enough to know they were dealing with a homicide.

———

The breakthrough came when child protection workers interviewed the surviving children in the home. Away from Brett and Sarah's intimidating presence, the kids revealed the horrific truth about life in the apartment.

Brent and Sarah Hallow

Autumn's six-year-old brother spoke in the matter-of-fact way children describe even the most abnormal situations. He told investigators about the brown belt with lace ends that Brett and Sarah used to tie Autumn up. He described how they would zip her into the red sleeping bag with only her head sticking out, then leave her restrained overnight as punishment.

He explained that this happened whenever Autumn was "being bad," which meant whenever she wet herself or tried to get food when she was hungry. He had watched his sister being systematically tortured and had been powerless to help her.

Sarah's ten-year-old daughter corroborated everything. She, too, had witnessed the restraints, the starvation, and the endless cycle of punishment for behaviors that were actually signs of severe distress.

Most damaging of all, the boy described what he had heard on the morning Autumn died: both adults in the bathroom with his sister, followed by her screaming and a loud bang.

When investigators searched the apartment, they found the brown belt and red sleeping bag exactly as the children had described them.

———

The medical examiner's findings destroyed any remaining doubt about what had happened to Autumn. She had died from asphyxial injuries combined with blunt force trauma. She had been strangled or suffocated while also suffering violent impacts to her body. There was no water in her lungs, definitively disproving the drowning claim.

The autopsy revealed the full extent of her suffering. Internal bleeding in her abdomen and brain showed she had been struck repeatedly. The puncture wounds on her forehead likely came from the belt's hardware being pressed into her skin during restraint. Every injury told the story of a prolonged, sadistic assault.

Additional evidence painted an even darker picture. The surveillance footage recovered from the apartment showed not just the final assault, but months of previous abuse. Brett and Sarah had documented their own crimes, creating a video record of their escalating violence toward a helpless child.

Investigators determined that Autumn had likely been dead for much longer than Sarah claimed. The condition of her body suggested she might have died a full day before the 911 call, meaning Brett and Sarah had spent hours with her corpse while deciding how to stage the scene.

———

On August 17, 2020, Brett Jason Hallow and Sarah K. Hallow were formally charged with second-degree murder and first-degree manslaughter. The charges reflected not just Autumn's death, but the ongoing pattern of child abuse that had led to it.

Both initially pleaded not guilty, perhaps hoping their drowning story might create reasonable doubt. However, as prosecutors assembled their case with medical evidence, video footage, and witness testimony from the surviving children, the weight of the evidence became overwhelming.

On June 21, 2021, nearly a year after Autumn's death, both defendants accepted plea agreements. Standing before Judge Karen Schommer, they admitted to the systematic torture and murder of an eight-year-old girl who should have been under their protection.

Sarah Hallow testified through tears, acknowledging that she and Brett had repeatedly assaulted Autumn in the bathroom during her final days. She admitted they had confined the child, withheld food and water, and denied her medical care. It was a confession to torture in all but name.

Brett Hallow spoke less, but his guilty plea served as an admission to everything prosecutors had alleged. The man who should have been Autumn's protector had instead become her tormentor.

———

On September 23, 2021, Judge Schommer sentenced both Brett and Sarah Hallow to forty years in prison—the maximum penalty under their plea agreement. The judge cited the "particular cruelty" of their actions in justifying the harsh sentence.

In court, Kelsey Kruse delivered a victim impact statement that left observers in tears. She described visiting Autumn's body at the funeral home and struggling to recognize her own daughter. The child's head had been shaved due to injuries to her scalp, her shoulders looked impossibly small, and marks covered her face.

"The hardest part is not that my daughter is dead," Kelsey said. "It's how she died, how she suffered."

Autumn's older brother, then eleven, had written his own statement that Kelsey read aloud: "Even though I know they are locked up, I feel like my dad or Sarah is watching me through my bedroom window at night."

When given the opportunity to speak, Sarah offered a tearful apology that many found hollow. Brett remained silent, offering no explanation or expression of remorse for destroying his daughter's life.

The sentences meant both would spend the majority of their remaining adult lives behind bars. For Brett Hallow, it represented the ultimate betrayal—a father who had murdered the child he was supposed to love and protect.

————

Even as Brett and Sarah faced justice, questions remained about how the system had failed Autumn so completely. Thirty-one police calls to their apartment. Multiple reports of suspected abuse. A desperate mother begging for help. Medical professionals filing concerns with child protection.

The education system had also missed critical warning signs. School officials at Lincoln Elementary, where Autumn had just completed second grade, were aware of abuse within the family. A school health aide observed bruises covering Autumn's brother's body, and a school counselor received evidence of abuse from Kelsey but allegedly failed to make the required reports to authorities.

At every turn, agencies that were supposed to protect children had found reasons to look the other way. Officers accepted the Hallows' explanations. Child protection services closed cases without adequate investigation. The family court system dismissed a mother's fears as mere custody disputes.

Kelsey Kruse filed a thirty-million-dollar federal lawsuit against Sherburne County Child Protection Services and the Elk River Police Department, seeking accountability for the failures that cost her daughter's life. The suit detailed how repeated warnings were ignored, how welfare checks were conducted inadequately, and how a pattern of abuse was dismissed as family court matters.

The lawsuit represented more than just seeking damages—it was an attempt to force systemic changes that might prevent another child from suffering Autumn's fate.

———

Today, Autumn Hallow is remembered not for the way she died, but for the bright, creative child she was before the abuse began. Her family planted an Autumn Blaze maple tree in her memory, a living reminder of the girl who loved to draw, dance, and help others.

Kelsey Kruse started a tradition of performing random acts of kindness on Fridays in Autumn's honor, channeling her grief into positive action. "I feel like I'm still her mom," she said, "so I'm still taking care of her."

CHAPTER 4

THE DIGITAL TRAIL

Taylor Behl had been counting down the days until college for months. At seventeen, she radiated an excitement that seemed to bubble up from somewhere deep inside her. Her parents, Janet and Matt, had divorced when she was young, but they had maintained a cordial relationship centered around their only daughter. Taylor split her time between her mother's home in Vienna, Virginia, and her father's place in Springfield, but regardless of where she stayed, she was always planning her next adventure.

The summer of 2005 was filled with preparations for her freshman year at Virginia Commonwealth University. She visited the campus twice that spring, falling in love with the urban energy of Richmond. During her April visit, she stayed at her friend Mike Cino's apartment near campus. Mike was a year older and already settled into college life. What Taylor didn't realize was that this visit would introduce her to someone who would alter the trajectory of her young life in ways she could never imagine.

Mike's roommate was Benjamin Fawley. At thirty-eight, Ben seemed oddly out of place in a college apartment, but he had a way of fitting into younger crowds that was both impressive and unsettling. He was tall and lanky, with an almost boyish face that made him appear younger than his years. Ben told people he was an amateur photographer with an interest in gothic culture, and his online presence reflected this carefully crafted persona. He maintained several websites and blogs dedicated to skulls, dark art, and what he called his "goth lifestyle."

His apartment was a shrine to death. Skulls lined the shelves —some real, some sculpted by his own hands during long nights when sleep wouldn't come. License plates covered nearly every available inch of wall space, collected from sources he never fully explained. His photography equipment was always within reach, ready to capture images of the young women he convinced to pose for him under the guise of building their modeling portfolios.

During that April visit, Taylor and Ben had a brief sexual encounter. According to her best friend, Glynnis, and her mother, Janet, Taylor described it as something she did "once out of curiosity." She found Ben's intensity unsettling afterward—the way he stared at her, the way he seemed to believe their brief encounter meant more than it did. But they continued to communicate online through MySpace and LiveJournal. Ben seemed to interpret their brief encounter as the beginning of something significant, while Taylor saw it as a mistake she preferred not to repeat.

Ben's life was far more complicated and dangerous than he let on to his young friends. He was a divorced father of two young daughters who lived with their mother in Pennsylvania. He survived on Social Security disability payments due to bipolar disorder and had a criminal history that read like a warning sign: convictions for assault, destruction of property, theft, and reckless endangerment. His ex-girlfriend from 2003 had learned firsthand about his capacity for violence when he was convicted of assaulting her.

But Taylor knew none of this dark history when she moved to Richmond in August 2005. She was focused on starting fresh, making new friends, and embracing her independence. Her roommate, Emma Ellsworth, seemed like a perfect match—another freshman navigating the transition to college life. Taylor's MySpace profile under the handle "tiabliaj" reflected her optimism, filled with photos and posts about her excitement for the future.

———

Monday, September 5, 2005, dawned hot and humid in Virginia. Taylor had spent the Labor Day weekend with her mother, Janet, in Vienna. The drive back to Richmond was routine—just over a hundred miles down Interstate 95, a journey she had made dozens of times during her campus visits.

She arrived at VCU in the early evening, the campus still quiet in the aftermath of the long weekend. At 6:44 p.m., she called her father, Matt, to let him know she had arrived safely. It was a responsible gesture, one that showed the thoughtful person Taylor had become.

At around 10:20 p.m., Taylor returned to her dorm room to find her roommate entertaining her boyfriend. With the thoughtfulness that characterized her, Taylor decided to give them privacy. She grabbed her car keys, cell phone, student

ID, and about forty dollars in cash. She told Emma she was going out and would be back in three hours.

"I'll just go skateboard for a while," she said, shouldering her backpack.

———

Tuesday, September 6, brought the first signs that something was terribly wrong. Taylor missed her classes—completely out of character for someone who had been so excited about starting college. Emma tried calling her throughout the day, but each call went straight to voicemail. Taylor's phone wasn't just turned off; it had gone completely dead.

By Tuesday evening, Emma was genuinely worried. She contacted campus security, but they told her she needed to wait twenty-four hours before filing a missing person report. The policy was standard procedure for dealing with college students who sometimes disappeared for a night or two.

While Emma was trying to report Taylor missing, Ben Fawley was at the Richmond Police Department filing a very different report. At 4:00 p.m. on Tuesday, Ben told officers that he had been the victim of a violent crime. According to his statement, at around 5:00 a.m. that morning, he had been walking through an alley near VCU when several men had attacked him. They had struck him in the stomach, thrown a bag over his head, and forced him into a vehicle.

Ben Fawley

The story Ben told was elaborate and detailed. The alleged kidnappers had driven him to a dirt road, stolen his camera equipment and about twenty dollars, and then dumped him before dawn. He described feeling disoriented and confused, unable to remember exactly how he had made it back to his apartment.

But the officer who took Ben's statement noticed troubling inconsistencies. Ben seemed to be off his psychiatric medication and appeared intoxicated. The details of his story were vague when they should have been specific, and detailed when they should have been vague. Ben couldn't describe his attackers' voices or provide any useful details about the vehicle or the location where he was allegedly dumped. Most suspicious of all, he had waited nearly eleven hours to report this supposedly traumatic assault.

Still, the report was filed, creating an official record that Ben Fawley had been the victim of a crime around the same time that Taylor Behl had gone missing.

————

At 1:00 a.m. on Wednesday, September 7, Taylor had been gone for more than twenty-four hours, and Emma finally convinced campus security to take an official missing person report. The university police began the process of notifying her parents and starting a preliminary investigation.

Janet Pelasara received the call in the middle of the night. The words every parent dreads hearing: Your child is missing. She immediately drove through the darkness from Vienna to Richmond, her hands gripping the steering wheel as her mind raced through possibilities. Matt Behl made the same journey, and by Wednesday morning, both parents were on campus, desperate for answers about their daughter's whereabouts.

The initial investigation moved with frustrating slowness. Campus police treated it as a routine missing person case, assuming Taylor would turn up with a reasonable explanation for her absence. They interviewed Emma and reviewed the basic facts: Taylor had left her dorm at around 10:30 p.m. on Monday to go out. She had taken her car keys, and both she and her car had vanished without a trace.

Friends and classmates rallied around the search effort. They created flyers with Taylor's photo and distributed them around campus and throughout Richmond. The images showed a beautiful young woman with shoulder-length blondish-brown hair and a bright smile—someone whose disappearance would capture public attention and generate hundreds of tips, most of them leading nowhere.

But as the days passed without any sign of Taylor, the case began to attract more serious attention from law enforcement. This wasn't a college student sleeping off a weekend bender. This was something much more sinister.

———

By September 11, six days after Taylor's disappearance, the VCU police department officially announced they were consulting with the FBI. An Amber Alert was issued for Taylor and her 1977 white Ford Escort. An eleven-person task force was formed, including local police, university security, state police, and federal investigators. The case was now being treated as a criminal investigation.

Investigators began the painstaking process of reconstructing Taylor's last days. They interviewed her friends, reviewed her cell phone records, and examined her computer with forensic software that was still relatively new in 2005. What they found was a digital trail that led them into the world of MySpace and online social networking—territory that was still relatively uncharted for law enforcement.

Taylor's MySpace profile revealed an active social life and numerous online friendships. However, it was the connections and communications they found there that began to point investigators toward their first real suspect. Ben Fawley's name appeared in Taylor's online friend list, and investigators discovered they had been communicating regularly.

As detectives dug deeper into their communications, a troubling picture emerged. Taylor had mentioned Ben to her friends, describing him as "weird" and someone she was trying to distance herself from. Her phone records showed that at 9:45 p.m. on September 5, she had made a brief call to an unidentified male friend. Then her phone had gone completely silent.

Ben's online persona was disturbing. He went by "Skulz" or "skulz67" on various websites, maintaining several blogs and web pages dedicated to Gothic subculture, death imagery, and what he called his artistic vision. His photography galleries featured dozens of young women, many of them appearing to be college-aged or younger. The images weren't necessarily inappropriate, but there was something unsettling about the collection—the sheer volume of young faces staring out from the screen.

When detectives looked deeper into Ben's background, red flags immediately appeared. His criminal history included multiple convictions for assault, theft, and destruction of property. His age—twenty-one years older than Taylor—raised questions about the nature of their relationship. His disability status and documented mental health issues painted a picture of someone who was potentially unstable but certainly capable of violence.

But Ben had an explanation for everything. When questioned by police, he readily admitted to seeing Taylor on the night she disappeared. He told investigators that she had come to his apartment at around 9:00 p.m. to borrow a skateboard. According to his story, he had then walked her back to her dorm at around 9:30 p.m. and left her there safely. He claimed he had no idea what happened to her after that.

The problem with Ben's story became apparent when investigators finally reviewed the security footage from Taylor's dormitory. The cameras told a different story entirely. At 10:21 p.m., Ben Fawley was recorded entering the building and pacing nervously in the lobby for three minutes—a man clearly agitated, checking his watch and running his hands through his hair. Then, at 10:24 p.m., Taylor appeared on camera, and they left together.

This revelation changed everything. Ben hadn't left Taylor safely at her dorm at 9:30 p.m. as he had claimed. He had been with her when she'd left the building for what would be her final journey.

Meanwhile, Ben's alleged assault on Tuesday morning was raising its own questions. His story about being kidnapped and robbed seemed increasingly unlikely as investigators examined the details. The timing of the alleged assault—just hours after Taylor disappeared—seemed too coincidental to believe.

On September 8, Ben posted about the supposed attack on his LiveJournal, speculating that an angry ex-girlfriend might have orchestrated it. But strangely, he never mentioned Taylor's disappearance in the post, despite claiming to be her friend.

On September 10, Ben made another cryptic post: "I lost a skateboard the other day." Investigators wondered if this referred to the skateboard he claimed to have lent Taylor.

———

The breakthrough came at dawn on Saturday, September 17. An off-duty Richmond police officer was walking his dog through the Fan District when he noticed something that didn't belong. A white Ford Escort was parked on a quiet residential street, but it had Ohio license plates and a Vienna, Virginia parking sticker in the window. The combination didn't make sense, and the officer's instincts told him to investigate further.

He checked the vehicle identification number and felt his pulse quicken when he realized what he had found: Taylor's missing car.

But the license plates told a disturbing story. They didn't belong to Taylor—they had been stolen from another vehicle weeks earlier. Someone had deliberately swapped the plates, most likely to conceal the car's identity and delay its discovery. The implications were chilling: Whoever had taken Taylor's car had planned carefully, thinking through the steps needed to avoid detection.

Police immediately established surveillance on the vehicle, hiding officers in nearby locations and hoping whoever had left it there might return. For twelve hours, they watched and waited. Finally, with no activity and no sign of anyone returning, they impounded the vehicle for forensic examination.

The forensic team found evidence that would both advance and complicate the investigation. A police K-9 unit detected two distinct scent trails from the car. One was clearly Taylor's, which made sense since it was her vehicle. The second scent led investigators on a path several blocks away to a house on Sheppard Street, where a twenty-two-year-old man named Jesse Schultz lived with his aunt and uncle.

Jesse worked at The Village Café and was part of the skateboarding crowd that included many of Taylor's friends. However, when police questioned him, Jesse insisted he had never met Taylor and had never been in her car. His answers on a polygraph test came back as deceptive, leading to his arrest on drug possession charges.

But as investigators dug deeper, the evidence against Jesse began to unravel. They theorized that his scent might have transferred to Taylor's car indirectly, perhaps through a mutual friend who had been in both vehicles. Within days, Jesse was cleared as a suspect.

The discovery of the car had actually strengthened the case against Ben in several ways. The stolen Ohio plates were significant because Ben had once lived in Ohio and was known to collect license plates. The location where the car was found suggested someone familiar with Richmond's neighborhoods, while the timing of its placement indicated careful planning rather than panicked disposal.

———

On September 23, police arrested Ben Fawley, but not for Taylor's disappearance. During their investigation of his background and computer equipment, they had discovered something that gave them immediate leverage: Ben was in possession of child pornography. Sixteen separate charges were filed based on videos found on his computer, some involving children as young as one year old.

The discovery was sickening but strategically valuable. The child pornography charges ensured that Ben would remain in jail without bond while investigators continued building their case for Taylor's disappearance.

Ben's apartment was another disturbing glimpse into a troubled mind. The walls were covered with license plates—dozens of them, arranged in overlapping patterns that suggested obsessive behavior. Some were legitimate souvenirs, but others appeared to have been stolen, pried off vehicles in parking lots and driveways.

Among Ben's photography and computer files, investigators found numerous images he had taken over the years. Many were shots of young women he had convinced to model for him, often under the guise of building their portfolios. However, buried among hundreds of photos was one image that would change everything.

The photograph showed a rural scene—an old barn and weathered outbuildings surrounded by dense woods. It appeared to be in a remote location, accessible only by dirt roads.

Investigators showed this photo to people who knew Ben, hoping someone might recognize the location. For weeks, they came up empty. The image could have been taken anywhere in rural Virginia, and without more specific landmarks, it seemed like a dead end.

The breakthrough came from an unexpected source. Erin Crabill, one of Ben's ex-girlfriends, immediately recognized the scene when police showed her the photograph. The blood drained from her face as she realized what she was looking at.

"That's my family's property," she said, her voice barely above a whisper, "in Mathews County."

Ben had visited the property when they were dating, and he had apparently photographed it for reasons that were now becoming terrifyingly clear.

———

On October 5, 2005, one month after Taylor's disappearance, investigators made the seventy-five-mile drive to Mathews County. The property was exactly as it appeared in Ben's photograph—remote, wooded, and accessible only by winding dirt roads that seemed to lead nowhere.

In a wooded area behind the barn, about a hundred yards from the main structure, investigators found what they had been both seeking and dreading. In a shallow grave, hastily covered with dirt and forest debris, lay severely decomposed human remains.

The body was mostly skeletal, the soft tissue long since decomposed in the Virginia heat and humidity. What clothing remained was in tatters, but pieces of fabric matched the description of what Taylor had been wearing when she'd disappeared. The remains were partially unclothed, suggesting violence before death.

Most disturbing of all, the grave showed signs of hasty, panicked burial. It was shallow—barely three feet deep—and the body had been positioned awkwardly, as if the person who'd dug it had been in a desperate hurry. Scattered around the remains were pieces of duct tape and plastic material, suggesting the body had been wrapped or bound at some point.

The next day, October 6, dental records confirmed what everyone already knew: The remains were Taylor Behl's. After a month of desperate searching, her family finally had the terrible closure they had been seeking.

Dr. Marcella Fierro, Virginia's chief medical examiner, arrived to oversee the recovery and preliminary examination. The condition of the remains made determining a precise cause of death nearly impossible, but it was clear that the manner of death was homicide.

———

With Taylor's body discovered and the evidence mounting against him, Ben Fawley's story began to change dramatically. From his jail cell, he provided investigators with a new version of events that was even more disturbing than his original account.

According to Ben's latest story, he and Taylor had driven to Mathews County together on the night of September 5. He claimed they had consumed drugs and alcohol before engaging in consensual sex that involved "erotic asphyxiation"—a dangerous sexual practice that involves restricting oxygen to the brain.

Ben said he had placed a bag over Taylor's head during sex, and she had passed out and died accidentally. Panicking upon realizing she was dead, Ben claimed he had driven back to Richmond with Taylor's body in her car, then returned the next day to bury her in the remote location. He insisted it was a tragic accident, not murder.

But Ben's story had problems that went far beyond its inherent implausibility. The timeline didn't work. Taylor had been seen leaving her dorm at 10:24 p.m., which would have made a round trip to Mathews County and back nearly impossible, given when Ben reported his alleged assault on Tuesday morning.

More importantly, Ben's behavior after Taylor's supposed accidental death was completely inconsistent with someone dealing with a tragic accident. The fabricated assault report filed on Tuesday afternoon looked like a calculated attempt to establish an alibi. His decision to hide Taylor's car with stolen license plates suggested careful planning rather than a panicked reaction.

Even more damning, Ben had continued to participate in the search for Taylor, even showing up to help look for her while knowing exactly where her body was buried.

Then, while incarcerated, Ben made statements that completely undermined his accident story. He told a prison guard that his original statement about erotic asphyxiation was a lie, fabricated to "beat the system." In a letter to an ex-girlfriend, he wrote that he was "the reason Taylor was dead" and that he "deserved to be in prison."

These admissions painted a picture of a man who had deliberately killed Taylor, then concocted an elaborate cover story to avoid responsibility.

———

In January 2006, a Mathews County grand jury indicted Ben Fawley on charges of first-degree murder. The indictment alleged that Taylor had been killed "in the commission of, or attempt to commit, rape, forcible sodomy or abduction."

The charges could have made Ben eligible for the death penalty under Virginia law, but prosecutors chose to pursue first-degree murder rather than capital murder. As the case moved toward trial, prosecutors faced the challenge of proving murder without definitive physical evidence.

But on August 9, 2006, just one week before the trial was scheduled to begin, Ben Fawley made a decision that ended the case without a jury ever hearing the evidence. He entered an Alford plea to second-degree murder, meaning he didn't admit guilt but acknowledged that the prosecution had enough evidence to convict him.

Judge William H. Shaw III sentenced Ben to thirty years in prison, the maximum penalty for second-degree murder in Virginia. As part of the plea agreement, the sixteen child pornography charges were dropped.

During the sentencing hearing, Ben was seen sobbing and clutching photographs of his two young daughters. He offered no apology to Taylor's family.

Prosecutor Jack Gill rejected any suggestion that the case had been about consensual sex gone wrong. "Simply, this was a case about murder," he told the court, emphasizing that a vibrant young woman had been senselessly killed by someone who had preyed upon her youth and trust.

In the gallery, about thirty-five of Taylor's relatives and supporters watched as justice was finally served. Janet Pelasara, Taylor's mother, had remained composed through most of the proceedings, but as deputies led Ben away in handcuffs, her emotions erupted.

"Murderer!" she shouted at Ben's retreating figure.

It was a cathartic moment that captured the depth of the family's loss and their satisfaction that the man who had killed their daughter would finally pay for his crime.

———

Ben Fawley would be middle-aged to elderly upon release in 2031, and as a convicted killer, he would live under scrutiny for whatever remained of his life. His two young daughters would grow up knowing their father had committed an unthinkable crime.

For Taylor's family, the plea had spared them the ordeal of a trial, but it couldn't heal the wound of losing their daughter. Janet later said that no sentence could bring Taylor back or make the pain disappear.

The case marked one of the first times law enforcement had successfully used social media evidence to solve a major crime. Taylor's MySpace friends list had helped investigators narrow their suspect pool, and Ben's digital footprint had ultimately led them to her body. It was a preview of how criminal investigations would evolve in the internet age.

Erin Crabill, Ben's ex-girlfriend who had recognized the photograph, received a twenty-thousand-dollar reward that had been offered for information leading to Taylor's discovery. She used part of the money to establish a fund for women in crisis, ensuring that even in tragedy, Taylor's memory would help others.

Taylor would have turned eighteen just one week after her body was discovered. Instead of celebrating her birthday and embracing adulthood, her family held her funeral, laying to rest a young woman whose life had been cut short just as it was beginning to bloom.

CHAPTER 5

A SHOT IN THE DARK

Janice Trahan had always believed in the nobility of healing. As a young nurse at Lafayette General Hospital in Louisiana, she took pride in her work, caring for patients with a dedication that earned respect from colleagues and physicians alike. The hospital corridors were her domain—a place where she felt confident and capable, and where her skills could make a real difference in people's lives.

She was twenty-one when she first met Dr. Richard Schmidt in 1984, a married gastroenterologist with three children who commanded attention wherever he went. Richard was charming in the way that successful doctors often are—confident, articulate, and devoted to his patients. He had a way of making everyone around him feel important, and Janice was no exception.

What began as professional respect gradually evolved into something more complicated. Richard would find reasons to seek out Janice's assistance, praising her nursing skills and asking for her input on patient care. Their conversations lingered longer than necessary, and soon Richard was inviting himself into Janice's personal life. Richard had a way of making Janice feel seen in ways she had never experienced before.

The attention was intoxicating. Richard would show up at Janice's family gatherings, charming her relatives with stories from his medical practice. He integrated himself seamlessly into her world, making promises that seemed both thrilling and impossible.

"I'm going to leave my wife," Richard confided during one of their private conversations. "We could have a real life together, Janice. A real family."

The words hung between them like a secret that could change everything.

————

By 1985, Janice had made a decision that would alter the course of her life. Believing in Richard's promises, she divorced her first husband and committed herself fully to their relationship. Richard painted vivid pictures of their future together—a life where they wouldn't have to hide, where their love could exist in the open.

But months passed, and Richard remained married. There was always another excuse, another delay. "After the holidays," he would say, or "once things settle down at the practice." The promises became a familiar refrain, always just out of reach.

————

When Janice became pregnant in early 1991, she thought it might finally force Richard to make good on his word. Surely a child would be the catalyst that pushed him to leave his wife and start their new life together.

Instead, Richard's reaction revealed a side of him that Janice had only glimpsed before. The controlling tendencies that had seemed protective now felt suffocating.

"Remove my name from the birth certificate," Richard demanded after their son was born in March. "It's too complicated right now. People might ask questions."

Janice complied, though the request broke her heart. Richard provided child support of $300 to $500 a month, but always with the reminder that this arrangement was temporary, just until he could properly leave his wife.

But Richard never left his wife. The excuses continued, and Janice began to see the pattern for what it really was. Richard didn't want to choose between his two lives; he wanted to control both completely.

The control extended far beyond broken promises. Richard became increasingly possessive, monitoring Janice's activities and relationships. He refused to use protection during their encounters, leading to multiple pregnancies that he pressured Janice to terminate. When she tried to date other men during their periodic separations, Richard would intervene with threatening phone calls.

"Stay away from my woman," he would tell her suitors, his voice carrying a menace that left no room for argument.

Richard made his expectations clear to Janice as well. If she ever tried to leave him permanently, there would be consequences. He threatened to post compromising photographs of her around the hospital. He would destroy her nursing career. He would make sure no man would ever want her again.

"He's going to end up killing me," Janice confided to family members during particularly difficult periods. Richard's threats felt real, and his volatile behavior suggested he was capable of following through on them.

For nearly a decade, this cycle continued. Janice found herself trapped between hope and fear, unable to fully break free from Richard's influence yet increasingly aware that his promises were empty. She was thirty-one years old, and she could see her life slipping away in service to Richard's ego and manipulation.

By the summer of 1994, Janice had finally reached her breaking point. The realization finally hit her: Richard would never leave his wife. He would never choose her over his comfortable, established life. The promises that had sustained her for ten years were nothing more than tools of control.

In July 1994, Janice made a definitive decision. The affair was over. She stopped taking Richard's calls, refused his visits, and began the serious work of building a life without him.

Richard didn't take the rejection well.

———

The late-night visit came on August 4, 1994. Janice had been sleeping peacefully beside her three-year-old son when she heard Richard's voice calling her name from the doorway of her bedroom. She woke to find him standing over her bed, syringe in hand.

"You need another B-12 shot," Richard said, his voice carrying an urgency that seemed out of place for a routine vitamin injection. "It'll help with your energy levels."

"This can wait until morning," Janice protested groggily, but Richard was insistent. In the dim light of her bedroom, she could barely make out his familiar silhouette as he prepared the injection.

Dr. Richard Schmidt

The needle slid into her arm, and Janice knew something was wrong immediately. The injection burned with an intensity she had never experienced before. It was nothing like the routine B-12 shots Richard had given her in the past; pain shot down her entire arm like fire through her veins.

Before she could fully process what had happened, Richard was already moving toward the door.

"I have an emergency at Hamilton Medical Center," he said quickly, his voice carrying an unusual tension. "I have to go."

And then he was gone, leaving Janice alone in the darkness with a throbbing arm and a growing sense that something was terribly wrong.

Unable to shake her unease, Janice decided to verify Richard's story. She called Hamilton Medical Center's emergency room, asking if Dr. Schmidt was there attending to a patient. The response confused her—there was no Dr. Schmidt at the hospital that night. No emergency involving him. No record of his presence anywhere in the building.

Janice immediately paged Richard. When he called back, it was obvious he wasn't calling from a hospital. The background noise, the quality of the connection—everything suggested he was calling from his office or home.

"I thought you were at Hamilton Medical," Janice said.

Richard's explanation was fumbling and unconvincing. He claimed he had been on a different floor, that the emergency room staff wouldn't necessarily know he was there. But Janice could hear the lie in his voice, and she pressed him about the unusual pain from the injection.

"I'm sorry," Richard said, his voice carrying an odd tone she'd never heard before. "I promise I'll never give you another shot in the dark."

The phrase stuck with her. *Shot in the dark.* Why would he phrase it that way? Why apologize so profusely for what should have been a routine vitamin injection?

Within days of the injection, Janice began experiencing symptoms that alarmed her. It started with fatigue—a bone-deep exhaustion that no amount of sleep could cure. Then came the swollen lymph nodes in her neck and head, followed by a persistent sore throat and mouth ulcers that made eating painful.

She confided in a colleague at Lafayette General about the strange late-night injection and Richard's suspicious behavior afterward. Something was wrong, she was certain of it, and she wanted someone else to know what had happened in case her health took a sudden turn.

———

As weeks passed, the symptoms intensified rather than improved. Janice found herself visiting doctor after doctor, each one puzzled by her condition. The symptoms suggested a viral infection, but nothing specific could be identified.

On August 12, eight days after the injection, Janice had an appointment with Richard himself. Despite everything, she still saw him as her physician, and she hoped he might have insights into her declining health. Richard drew her blood for testing, later telling her that everything looked normal except for a slightly low white blood cell count, which he attributed to a minor virus.

Throughout the fall of 1994, Janice's health continued to deteriorate. She saw a neurologist for severe headaches, an optometrist for eye pain and fatigue, and an ear, nose, and throat specialist who performed a lymph node biopsy in September. The biopsy showed a reactive viral infection— clear evidence that her body was fighting some kind of virus —but doctors couldn't identify what it was.

Behind the scenes, Richard was actively interfering with Janice's medical care. When she was referred to an oncologist because of concerns about lymphoma, Richard called the doctor before the appointment. He told the oncologist that he suspected Janice had a viral infection and claimed that certain tests had already been performed with negative results. Based on Richard's professional opinion, the oncologist didn't order additional testing.

By November, Janice's dentist was noticing troubling signs— inflamed gums, swollen lymph nodes, and abnormal blood counts that suggested her immune system was severely compromised. Still, no one could determine what was causing her illness.

————

The breakthrough came in December 1994, almost five months after the injection. Janice visited her OB/GYN, Dr. Wayne Daigle, who had delivered her son with Richard and was aware of their complicated history. Dr. Daigle was alarmed by Janice's weight loss, persistent fatigue, and ongoing viral symptoms.

He ran a comprehensive panel of tests, initially suspecting hepatitis. However, something made him add additional testing to the order—call it medical intuition or thoroughness, but that decision would change everything.

On December 20, 1994, the lab called Dr. Daigle with results that sent a chill through his office. The test he had added—an HIV test—had come back positive.

Dr. Daigle stared at the lab report, trying to process what he was seeing. Janice was a thirty-two-year-old nurse with no known risk factors for HIV. She wasn't an intravenous drug user, had no history of unsafe sexual practices, and had never had an occupational exposure to the virus at the hospital. How had a healthy young woman suddenly contracted HIV?

Knowing how devastating this news would be, Dr. Daigle made the difficult decision to wait until after the holidays to tell Janice. On January 3, 1995, he gently broke the news that would shatter her world.

The diagnosis hit Janice like a physical blow. HIV in 1995 was still largely considered a death sentence, and she struggled to understand how this could have happened to her. But as the initial shock wore off, her mind began working through the possibilities.

She had been a regular blood donor with no history of infection. She had no occupational exposures at the hospital. Her recent sexual partners could be tested to rule out transmission through normal contact. As she eliminated each possibility, one explanation kept surfacing—that strange injection on August 4th.

Janice's first reaction wasn't disbelief or denial—it was immediate clarity. Her mind flashed back to that August night, to Richard's strange behavior, to the burning injection that felt so different from every other B-12 shot she'd received. In that moment, everything clicked into place.

Additional testing revealed that Janice had also contracted hepatitis C, another blood-borne virus, around the same time period. The coincidence was too striking to ignore.

"I believe I was inoculated with HIV by Dr. Richard Schmidt," she told investigators. The man who had threatened to make sure no other man would ever want her had apparently made good on his promise, but in a way more sinister than she had ever imagined.

———

When Janice walked into the Lafayette Police Department in early 1995, her accusation seemed almost impossible to prove. How do you investigate a crime where the weapon is invisible and the evidence exists at a molecular level?

Detective James Craft took on the case, immediately recognizing the challenges ahead. Janice's story was compelling, but proving that Richard had deliberately infected her would require evidence that had never been used in a criminal case before.

The first step was establishing a timeline and an opportunity. Janice had been a regular blood donor, and investigators obtained records showing that a donation she gave in April 1994, just months before the incident, tested negative for both HIV and hepatitis C. This proved she had been healthy leading up to the injection.

Investigators also contacted Janice's recent sexual partners, asking them to be tested. Her ex-husband, her new boyfriend, and every other man she had been intimate with in the relevant time period tested negative. The statistical probability that she had contracted HIV through normal sexual contact was virtually zero.

But Detective Craft needed more than circumstantial evidence. On July 13, 1995, he obtained search warrants for Richard's medical office, his home, and a sample of his blood. The timing was carefully planned—investigators waited until the end of the business day, allowing Richard to see his patients before executing the search after hours.

Richard's initial cooperation was superficial at best. When confronted about his relationship with Janice, he minimized it, claiming it had been brief and that he had discarded any mementos from their time together. He protested the blood draw, worried it would ruin his medical practice, but the warrant gave investigators the authority they needed.

When asked for Janice's patient file, Richard claimed he hadn't treated her since 1990. It was a quick lie that was immediately exposed when investigators opened her chart to find lab results from August 1994—clear evidence that he had been involved in her medical care at the exact time of the alleged crime.

———

The most damning evidence came from an unexpected source: Richard's own record-keeping system. His medical practice maintained spiral notebooks to log every blood draw performed in the office. Each entry typically included the date, patient name, tests ordered, and a lab accession number for tracking results.

Detective Craft noticed that one of these logbooks was missing from the shelf. Two notebooks were found easily— one covering March through December 1993, another covering August 15, 1994, through July 1995. Notably, the volume that should have covered December 1993 through August 14, 1994, was nowhere to be seen.

When questioned about the missing logbook, Richard feigned ignorance, but Detective Craft wasn't convinced. He expanded his search to a cluttered storage room at the back of the office, methodically going through boxes of old records.

Hidden in a box labeled "1982 records," buried under files a decade old, Craft found the missing logbook. It was the only item from the 1990s mixed in with otherwise ancient documents—a clear attempt at concealment.

The recovered logbook provided the smoking gun investigators needed. The entries ran chronologically from December 14, 1993, up through August 4, 1994—and then stopped abruptly, with all remaining pages blank.

Detective Craft focused on the final entries: August 2 and August 4, 1994. Unlike every other entry in the book, which listed specific lab tests and had numbered tracking stickers, these two entries were anomalous. The August 2 entry was for a patient identified as "L.L." and bore the cryptic note "(Purple Top for Dr.)" with no test or lab number recorded. The August 4 entry—the very last in the book—named a patient "D.M." and read "Lavender stopper for Dr. S." with no lab work indicated.

In other words, on those two specific dates, blood samples had been drawn and set aside for the doctor's personal use, not for any diagnostic testing. Every other blood draw in months of records had corresponding lab work. These two did not.

————

Detective Craft quickly identified the patients behind the initials. "L.L." was Leslie Louviere, a woman being treated by Richard for hepatitis C. "D.M." was Donald McClelland, an HIV-positive patient with full-blown AIDS who was under the care of an HIV specialist.

The significance was chilling. Richard had drawn blood from a hepatitis C patient on August 2, 1994, and from an AIDS patient on August 4, 1994—the very same day he had visited

Janice Trahan. These were exactly the two viruses Janice had contracted.

When investigators interviewed Leslie Louviere, she confirmed that on August 2, Richard had personally requested an extra blood sample during her visit. He told her he was conducting a "private study" on hepatitis C and promised not to charge her for the additional draw. His nurse took the blood sample, but when Leslie returned for her next appointment months later and asked about the study, Richard claimed he hadn't found anything significant and dropped the subject entirely.

Donald McClelland's story was equally revealing. On August 4, he had visited Richard's office for what was supposed to be a routine appointment in preparation for a medical procedure. Richard specifically requested an unplanned blood test, drawing a vial of McClelland's blood and giving him a vitamin B-12 shot.

Richard's billing records showed that a "drawing fee" was initially marked for McClelland's visit, then crossed out—as if someone was trying to erase the paper trail of the blood draw.

Neither blood sample had been sent to any laboratory. Instead, Richard had apparently kept them for a more sinister purpose.

———

With physical evidence of the blood draws and a clear timeline established, investigators faced their biggest challenge: proving scientifically that the blood Richard had taken from his patients was indeed the source of Janice's infections.

In 1995, using viruses as forensic evidence was uncharted territory. No one had ever been convicted in a criminal court based on genetic analysis of pathogens. The Louisiana authorities enlisted cutting-edge science, bringing in researchers to perform a phylogenetic analysis of the HIV strains.

The concept was revolutionary but logical. HIV mutates rapidly, and each infected person carries a unique viral "signature." By comparing the genetic sequence of HIV found in Janice's blood to the HIV from Donald McClelland, then contrasting both to unrelated HIV samples from the local community, scientists could determine whether Janice's virus came from McClelland.

The testing process was meticulous. Blood samples from Janice and McClelland were analyzed alongside approximately thirty other HIV-positive samples from the Lafayette area. Using viral RNA sequencing, researchers examined the genetic code of the virus from each sample, looking for patterns of similarity and difference.

The results were stunning. Janice's HIV strain was almost an exact match to McClelland's strain, with far fewer genetic differences than seen in any other comparison. Some viral sequences were identical between the two samples—a phenomenon that indicated one virus was directly descended from the other.

Statistically, the odds of such a close match occurring by coincidence were astronomically small. Of all the HIV samples tested, only Janice's and McClelland's showed this level of genetic similarity.

The hepatitis C evidence was equally compelling. Janice had contracted hepatitis C around the same time as HIV, despite having no risk factors for that virus either. Richard's records showed he had drawn blood from Leslie Louviere, a hepatitis C patient, just two days before taking McClelland's HIV-positive blood.

These were the only two instances in all of Richard's medical records where blood was drawn from patients but never sent for laboratory testing. The pattern was unmistakable—he had procured a deadly cocktail of viruses specifically to inject into Janice.

———

On July 23, 1996, nearly two years after the crime, Dr. Richard Schmidt was arrested and charged with attempted second-degree murder. The news sent shockwaves through Lafayette and beyond. A respected physician using HIV as a weapon was unprecedented, and the case quickly attracted national media attention.

Television programs and news outlets covered the story extensively. Richard's mugshot appeared in newspapers across the country, often accompanied by headlines dubbing it the "Doctor AIDS case." For his family, the publicity was devastating—his eldest daughter later recalled learning about her father's arrest from television news.

But Richard maintained his innocence throughout the legal proceedings. His defense team challenged every aspect of the case, particularly the novel genetic evidence. They argued that phylogenetic analysis was too experimental to be trusted in a criminal trial—that the science was unproven and potentially unreliable.

The defense also suggested alternative explanations for Janice's infection. Perhaps she had been infected by an undisclosed sexual partner, they argued, or through an accidental occupational exposure at the hospital. They pointed out that she worked around patients, raising the remote possibility of needle-stick injuries or blood contact.

————

When the case went to trial in the fall of 1998, it became a media sensation in Lafayette. The prosecution presented the timeline of Richard's relationship with Janice, the threats he had made, and the compelling scientific evidence linking him to her infection.

Janice took the stand to recount the decade-long affair and the ominous "shot in the dark" that had changed her life forever. She described Richard's controlling behavior, his threats to ruin her career and reputation if she ever left him, and the unusual pain of that August injection.

The scientific testimony was complex but powerful. Experts explained how Janice's HIV strain matched Donald McClelland's to a degree that was statistically almost impossible unless one had come from the other. The case marked the first time viral RNA had been used to prove a connection between individuals in a U.S. criminal trial.

Richard chose not to testify in his own defense. His only alibi witness was his wife, who testified that Richard was home on the night of August 4, 1994—except for an unexplained twenty-minute window when she was taking a bath and couldn't account for his whereabouts.

That brief gap was more than enough time for Richard to drive to Janice's house and administer the deadly injection.

————

On October 23, 1998, after just four hours of deliberation, the jury unanimously found Dr. Richard Schmidt guilty of attempted second-degree murder. The evidence, once laid out in its entirety, was overwhelming.

"I believe he's a very disturbed individual," one juror told reporters afterward. "He destroyed many lives, including his own."

In February 1999, the judge sentenced Richard Schmidt to the maximum penalty of fifty years in state prison. Given the calculated nature of the crime and Richard's abuse of his position as a physician, the court showed no leniency.

Richard surrendered his medical license and was led away to begin what was essentially a life sentence. He continued to protest his innocence, but he had become one of the first people—and certainly the first physician—to be convicted of using HIV as a weapon.

The case established important legal precedents for prosecuting deliberate disease transmission and opened the door for using genetic analysis of pathogens in criminal investigations. The methods pioneered in Richard's prosecution would later be used to solve other cases and even track bioterrorism threats.

———

For Janice, the conviction brought a measure of justice, but her battle was far from over. She married Jerry Allen in 1996, a man who stood by her through the ordeal and loved her despite the diseases Richard had inflicted upon her. Living with HIV and hepatitis C in the late 1990s meant a complex regimen of medications and constant medical monitoring, but Janice persevered.

Richard's appeals were unsuccessful. The Louisiana Court of Appeals upheld his conviction in 2000, the state supreme court denied his petition in 2001, and the U.S. Supreme Court refused to hear his case in 2002. When he became eligible for parole in 2015 after serving seventeen years, Janice appeared at the hearing to oppose his release. The parole board unanimously denied his request, noting that Richard continued to maintain his innocence and showed no remorse for his crimes.

On February 12, 2023, Dr. Richard Schmidt died in custody at age seventy-four while being treated at a prison hospital. He had spent nearly twenty-five years behind bars, never admitting to the crime that had destroyed so many lives.

Janice Trahan Allen outlived her attacker, passing away in October 2024. Through her courage in coming forward and testifying against Richard, she had helped establish crucial legal precedents and ensured that justice was served for one of the most unusual and disturbing crimes in medical history.

CHAPTER 6

THE SMOOTH TALKER

Anita Fagiani Andrews possessed a magnetic presence that drew people to her wherever she went. At fifty-one, she retained the poise and grace that had once made her a county fair beauty queen. Likewise, her warm smile and infectious laugh made her beloved among customers, whether she was working her day job at Napa State Hospital or tending the bar at the family establishment she'd inherited with her sister Muriel.

Fagiani's Cocktail Lounge sat on a quiet corner in Napa, California, a neighborhood tavern where regulars knew each other's names and troubles. Anita had thrown herself into running the place after her divorce, working double shifts to support her two children. She took pride in creating a welcoming atmosphere where locals could unwind after long days in the vineyards.

The evening of July 10, 1974, started like any other. Anita worked behind the bar, pouring drinks and chatting with customers as the sun set over the Napa Valley. The summer heat had finally broken, and a pleasant breeze drifted through the open windows. Most of the regulars had headed home by closing time, leaving just a handful of stragglers nursing their final drinks.

One patron caught Anita's attention that night—a stranger who'd been nursing a beer alone at the far end of the bar. He was middle-aged, perhaps in his late thirties, with dark hair and a disarming smile. He'd struck up conversations with other customers throughout the evening, displaying the smooth charm that came naturally to some men. There was something magnetic about him, the way he drew people in with stories and jokes.

But Anita noticed he seemed in no hurry to leave as closing time approached. While other customers settled their tabs and said their goodnights, the stranger lingered, smoking his cigarette and watching the room with sharp, calculating eyes.

As Anita began her closing routine—wiping down tables, washing glasses, and counting the till—the stranger remained at his stool. She felt increasingly uncomfortable with his presence but couldn't quite put her finger on why. He hadn't caused any trouble. He'd been polite, even charming. Yet something about the way he watched her made her skin crawl.

Finally, she approached him. "Last call was an hour ago," she said firmly. "I need to close up now."

The man smiled that disarming smile and stubbed out his cigarette in the ashtray. "Of course, darling. Just finishing up." He left money on the bar and headed toward the back of the establishment.

Anita felt her pulse quicken as she watched him disappear into the shadows. Something wasn't right. The way he moved, the calculating look in his eyes when he thought no one was watching—every instinct screamed danger.

She turned back to her closing duties, her hands trembling slightly as she wiped down the bar. The silence that followed felt oppressive, heavy with menace she couldn't yet understand. She strained to hear the back door open and close, but the sound never came.

The realization hit her: He was still in the building.

She never got the chance to call for help.

———

Muriel Fagiani arrived at the cocktail lounge early the next morning, keys jingling in her hand as she approached the front door. She and Anita had planned to inventory their liquor supply before the afternoon shift. The morning air still held a hint of coolness, though the day promised to be another scorcher.

She noticed immediately that something was wrong. Anita's car wasn't in its usual parking space behind the building. The back door, which should have been locked, stood slightly ajar.

"Anita?" Muriel called out as she stepped inside. Her voice echoed in the empty barroom. Beer glasses sat unwashed on the bar, and the cash register drawer hung open, its contents scattered.

A chill ran down Muriel's spine as she moved deeper into the building. "Anita, are you here?"

The silence was deafening.

Muriel pushed open the door to the back storeroom and screamed.

Her sister lay crumpled on the floor in a pool of dark blood, a screwdriver protruding from her torso. Anita's clothing was torn and disheveled, her body positioned in a way that suggested a sexual assault.

Muriel stumbled backward, bile rising in her throat as she reached for the phone with shaking fingers. The 911 operator's voice seemed to come from far away as she struggled to form coherent words through her hysteria.

"My sister... please... there's so much blood..."

Through her shock and grief, one detail registered with crystal clarity: The cash register had been emptied, but this wasn't about money. The savage brutality of the attack spoke to something far more sinister; this was the work of someone who enjoyed inflicting pain.

———

Napa County Sheriff's deputies arrived within minutes of Muriel's frantic 911 call. The small city of Napa rarely saw violent crime, and news of the murder sent shockwaves through the tight-knit community.

Detective Frank Rutledge took charge of the investigation. A twenty-year veteran, he'd seen his share of homicides, but the savagery of this attack unsettled him. The killer had used multiple weapons—the screwdriver for stabbing, a broken bottle for bludgeoning, and what appeared to be a knife for the throat wound. The level of violence suggested personal rage, yet Anita had no known enemies.

The crime scene yielded several promising clues. Fingerprints lifted from a beer bottle and the cash register might have belonged to the killer. A partial bloody fingerprint on the back staircase railing looked fresh. Most intriguingly, a cigarette butt sat in an ashtray on the bar—clearly not one of Anita's, as she didn't smoke.

Rutledge interviewed Muriel and other family members, looking for anyone who might have wanted to harm Anita. They described a woman beloved by her community, devoted to her children, and hardworking and kind. She'd had no romantic entanglements since her divorce, no business disputes, and no threats or angry customers.

"She was the sweetest person you'd ever meet," Muriel told the detective through her tears. "Everyone loved Anita. I can't imagine who would do this to her."

The investigation expanded to regular customers at the lounge, but again, everyone spoke of Anita with genuine affection and respect. No one could think of a reason someone would want to hurt her.

As days turned to weeks, the case began to stagnate. The fingerprints yielded no matches in the limited databases available in 1974. DNA analysis didn't exist yet, rendering the cigarette butt useless for identification purposes. Anita's stolen Cadillac Eldorado never surfaced, despite an APB issued throughout California and neighboring states.

Rutledge worked the case for months, following every lead and interviewing every potential witness. Unfortunately, without a suspect or physical evidence that could be processed with 1970s technology, the investigation gradually went cold.

The murder of Anita Andrews joined the growing backlog of California unsolved case files.

———

Three weeks after Anita's murder, Michelle Wallace was preparing for the adventure of a lifetime. The twenty-five-year-old photographer had just landed her first professional job in North Carolina and planned to celebrate with a solo hiking trip through the Colorado Rockies. Her friends thought she was crazy to venture into the wilderness alone, but Michelle thrived on independence and adventure.

She'd grown up in Illinois, the daughter of George and Margaret Wallace, who'd instilled in her a love of the outdoors and photography. Michelle saw the world through her camera lens, capturing beauty in landscapes and moments others might overlook. Her portfolio was impressive enough to land the North Carolina position, a dream job that would launch her career.

"I'm not worried about her," George Wallace told friends when they expressed concern about Michelle's solo trip. "That girl has more courage and common sense than most men I know."

Michelle packed her red Mazda station wagon with camping gear, photography equipment, and supplies for her trip to the mountains. Her German Shepherd, Oki, would be her only companion—a loyal dog who'd traveled with her on previous adventures.

On a warm August morning in 1974, Michelle set out for the Rockies near Crested Butte, Colorado. The plan was simple: hike the high country for a few days, take photographs of the stunning alpine scenery, and return refreshed and ready for her new job.

She stopped in the small mountain town of Gunnison to grab supplies and check trail conditions. The locals she spoke with were friendly and helpful, typical of the warm hospitality she'd found throughout Colorado. Several people remembered the attractive young woman with long, braided hair, the camera, and the big dog, traveling alone but seemingly confident and well-prepared.

Michelle spent three glorious days in the mountains, hiking trails that wound through meadows carpeted with wildflowers and alongside crystal-clear streams. Her camera captured frame after frame of breathtaking vistas—shots she hoped to develop and display in her new studio in North Carolina.

On August 30, 1974, she packed up her campsite for the final time and headed back toward Gunnison. She was eager to get on the road back to North Carolina, excited about the new chapter awaiting her.

The drive back to town took her along winding mountain roads where she encountered two men standing beside a broken-down vehicle. One was a local ranch hand named Chuck Matthews, whom she'd met briefly in Gunnison. The other was a stranger—an older man who introduced himself as Roy.

Michelle, characteristically helpful, offered them a ride back to town.

What she didn't know was that she'd just invited death into her vehicle.

———

Roy Melanson possessed an unsettling charisma that drew people in before they realized their mistake. At thirty-seven, he'd perfected the art of manipulation, reading people quickly and telling them exactly what they wanted to hear.

To ranchers, he was an experienced cowhand looking for work. To women, he was a romantic drifter with fascinating stories from the road.

Roy Melanson

His criminal record stretched back decades—burglary, rape, assault—but Melanson had a talent for talking his way out of trouble or simply disappearing before consequences caught up with him. He'd served time in Texas prisons but always managed to get released early through a combination of good behavior and legal maneuvering.

In August 1974, Melanson had drifted into Gunnison County, Colorado, spinning tales about his ranching experience to anyone who'd listen. He'd managed to get hired by Frank Spadafora, a local sheep rancher who needed help with predator control. Melanson claimed expertise in hunting mountain lions and coyotes, though his actual skills were far more sinister.

During his stay in Gunnison, he'd also integrated himself into the life of Lucille Burton, a woman vacationing with her five daughters at a remote cabin. Melanson convinced Lucille he was a harmless drifter who could help with chores around the property. What she didn't realize was that he'd begun sexually assaulting her fourteen-year-old daughter, Sally, using a combination of threats and manipulation to keep the girl silent.

The night he met Chuck Matthews at the Columbine bar, Melanson was spinning another web of lies. He told Matthews about a cabin he supposedly owned and horses that needed tending. When Matthews offered to help, Melanson saw an opportunity to extend his cover story and perhaps find new victims to exploit.

The plan went awry when Matthews's car broke down on the mountain road, leaving both men stranded. Then, when Michelle Wallace stopped to offer assistance, Melanson recognized a golden opportunity.

Here was an attractive young woman traveling alone, with a nice vehicle and valuable equipment. Even better, she was trusting—exactly the trait Melanson exploited in his victims.

After Michelle dropped Chuck Matthews at the Columbine bar, she continued driving with Melanson as her only passenger. He likely spun some story about needing to get to his supposed cabin or retrieve his horses. Michelle, generous by nature, probably agreed to take him wherever he needed to go.

The remote mountain road stretched ahead of them, winding through dense forest where no one would hear her screams.

Melanson waited until they were miles from any witnesses before revealing his true nature.

———

When Michelle failed to call her parents as promised, George and Margaret Wallace immediately knew that something was wrong. Their daughter was responsible and reliable—she would never leave them worrying without good reason.

George contacted the Gunnison County Sheriff's Office, but authorities initially showed little concern. Young people often extended their trips or got distracted by new adventures. The fact that Michelle was an adult made it difficult to justify an immediate search.

But George Wallace was insistent. He knew his daughter better than anyone, and her silence was completely out of character. After several increasingly frantic phone calls, he convinced deputies to begin looking for her.

The search started with Michelle's planned hiking routes, but rangers found no sign of her or her red Mazda station wagon. Her campsite had been cleaned up and abandoned, with no indication of what direction she'd taken.

The first break came when a local rancher reported finding a German Shepherd on his property. The dog had been shot, apparently by someone who considered it a threat to livestock. When authorities checked the dog's tags, they confirmed it was Oki, Michelle's beloved companion.

The discovery of Oki's body transformed the case from a missing person investigation to a suspected homicide. Michelle never would have abandoned her dog, and she certainly wouldn't have allowed anyone to harm him.

Chuck Matthews heard about Michelle's disappearance on a local radio broadcast and immediately contacted authorities. He described the ride she'd given him and Roy, explaining that she'd continued driving with the stranger after dropping him off.

Matthews provided a description of Roy and mentioned that the man had claimed to be an experienced ranch hand looking for work. Local rancher Frank Spadafora confirmed he'd hired someone matching that description—Roy Melanson, who'd given his full name and background information.

Suddenly, investigators had a suspect and a timeline. Roy Melanson had been the last person seen with Michelle Wallace, and now both Michelle and her car were missing.

———

Two weeks later, Roy Melanson was sitting in a white Cadillac outside a high school in Pueblo, Colorado, when a detective noticed suspicious activity. The two men in the car appeared to be dealing drugs to students, prompting the officer to investigate.

When questioned, Melanson produced a Texas driver's license for identification. A computer malfunction prevented an immediate background check, so both men were released with warnings.

Hours later, however, when the computer system came back online, the background check revealed shocking information. Roy Melanson was wanted in Texas on rape charges, and he'd recently been identified as a suspect in a Colorado missing person case.

Police located and arrested Melanson quickly. A subsequent search of the Cadillac revealed a treasure trove of evidence linking him to Michelle Wallace's disappearance.

In the car's trunk, investigators found Michelle's backpack, containing her driver's license and personal belongings. They also discovered the registration papers for her red Mazda station wagon and a set of car keys that matched her vehicle.

Perhaps most importantly, they found a pawn shop receipt for Michelle's camera equipment. When investigators tracked down the camera and developed the film still inside, they discovered the final photos she'd taken—beautiful landscape shots from her hiking trip with Oki in the foreground, followed by more recent images that chilled them to the bone.

The final on the roll showed Roy Melanson himself, lying casually on a couch next to an unidentified young woman. The image had clearly been taken after Michelle's disappearance, indicating that Melanson had been using her camera.

When confronted with this evidence, Melanson admitted to knowing Michelle but denied harming her. He claimed she'd given him a ride and allowed him to borrow her car, spinning an elaborate lie about their supposed arrangement.

Investigators weren't buying his story, but they faced a significant problem: Without Michelle's body or a clear crime scene, they couldn't prove she'd been murdered. The evidence strongly suggested foul play, but circumstantial evidence wouldn't be enough for a murder conviction.

Instead, prosecutors charged Melanson with vehicle theft, check fraud, and possession of stolen property related to Michelle's belongings. It wasn't justice for what they believed he'd done, but it would keep him behind bars while they continued searching for Michelle's body.

————

Roy Melanson was extradited to Texas to face the outstanding rape charges that had triggered his arrest. In 1975, he was convicted and sentenced to life in prison, effectively removing him from circulation while the Michelle Wallace case remained unsolved.

For George and Margaret Wallace, the lack of resolution proved devastating. Margaret fell into a deep depression, unable to cope with not knowing what had happened to her daughter. Six weeks after Michelle's disappearance, she took her own life, leaving a note requesting to be buried next to Michelle if her remains were ever found.

George was left to grieve alone, holding on to the hope that someday he'd learn the truth about Michelle's fate. He kept in touch with investigators over the years, always asking if there were any new developments in the case.

Meanwhile, in a Texas prison, Roy Melanson served his time and worked the appeals system. In the early 1980s, he managed to get his life sentence reduced, making him eligible for parole. Prison officials noted his generally good behavior, though he was a suspect in the death of a fellow inmate.

In March 1988, after serving only thirteen years, Roy Melanson was paroled and walked out of prison a free man.

————

Freedom didn't reform Roy Melanson—it simply gave him new opportunities to prey on victims. Within months of his release, he'd established himself in Port Arthur, Texas, renting a room from a kind-hearted landlady named Pauline Klumpp.

Pauline was fifty-one years old, responsible, and well-liked in her community. She owned the house where Melanson lived and treated her tenants fairly, even going so far as to lend them household items when needed.

In late June 1988, Pauline stopped by the rental house to retrieve a television she'd loaned to Melanson and to ask for his help fixing her air conditioner. It was the kind of neighborly interaction that happened every day in small communities across America.

Pauline was seen leaving with Melanson that day, and she was never seen again.

Her husband, who worked out of town during the week, became concerned when he couldn't reach her by phone. When he returned home, he found an ominous scene: a pot of gumbo still simmering on the stove, ruined after cooking unattended for days.

Pauline had clearly expected to return home quickly. She never would have left food cooking if she'd planned to be away.

Four days after her disappearance, police found Pauline's car abandoned in a parking lot behind a local grocery store. The television she'd gone to retrieve was still in the back seat. There was no sign of Pauline herself.

Investigators immediately focused on Roy Melanson as their prime suspect, but once again, he'd vanished. By the time they went looking for him, he'd already left Texas and was moving on to his next hunting ground.

————

Walker, Louisiana, was a small town where people still felt safe running errands alone after dark. Charlotte Sauerwin certainly felt no sense of danger when she stopped at the local laundromat on the evening of August 5, 1988.

At twenty-four, Charlotte was building a future with her fiancé, Vincent LeJeune. They'd been carefully saving money to buy land where they could build their first home together, planning every detail of the life they'd create as husband and wife.

As Charlotte waited for her clothes to wash, she struck up a conversation with other customers about her excitement over their savings plan. It was innocent small talk—friendly chatter that made waiting more bearable.

An older man sitting nearby seemed particularly interested in their conversation. He was smooth and charming, with a confident smile that drew people in. When Charlotte mentioned their plans to buy land, the stranger perked up with obvious interest.

He introduced himself as a land developer who happened to have property available at well below market value. What a coincidence! He'd be happy to show Charlotte and her fiancé some options that might be perfect for their needs.

Charlotte was intrigued. Land prices had been climbing steadily, and the idea of getting a good deal was appealing. When the stranger offered to drive her to see one of the properties right away, she agreed.

It was a decision that would cost Charlotte her life.

The property the stranger wanted to show her was remote and isolated, far from any witnesses who might hear her screams. Once he had Charlotte alone, Roy Melanson revealed his true nature.

He attacked her with savage brutality, raping and torturing her before wrapping a strap around her neck and strangling her. In a final act of violence, he slashed her throat with a blade, ensuring she couldn't survive to identify him.

Melanson dumped Charlotte's body in some brush near an old shed, taking her purse, jewelry, and the .380 caliber pistol she'd carried for protection. Then he disappeared into the night, leaving behind another devastated family and another unsolved murder.

———

Charlotte Sauerwin's body was discovered the next morning by a passerby who spotted her remains in the wooded area where Melanson had dumped her. The brutality of the attack shocked investigators—the strap was still wrapped around her neck, and the throat wound was so deep it had nearly decapitated her.

Witnesses from the laundromat described the middle-aged man who'd been talking to Charlotte, but their descriptions were vague. He'd been charming and well-spoken, driving a light-colored car with out-of-state license plates. Beyond that, they had little to offer investigators.

The case might have remained unsolved indefinitely, but Roy Melanson's arrogance was his downfall. In January 1989, he was arrested in Kentucky on weapons charges, caught carrying a firearm with a filed-off serial number.

The light-colored Chevrolet he was driving had Texas plates, matching the general description from the Sauerwin case. More significantly, the .380 caliber handgun in his possession would eventually be linked to Charlotte through the serial number.

Melanson served a short sentence in Kentucky for the weapons violation, then was arrested again in 1992 for burglary charges. This time, he wouldn't see freedom again.

———

In August 1992, volunteers from NecroSearch International combed a steep, rocky slope in the Colorado mountains, searching for remains that had been missing for eighteen years. The team included archaeologists, anthropologists, and other scientists who specialized in locating clandestine graves.

The search had been organized by detective Kathy Young, who'd reopened the Michelle Wallace case in 1989. Something about the case had captured her imagination—perhaps the senseless loss of such a young, vibrant woman, or the decades of grief endured by Michelle's family.

Young had sent hair samples from Michelle's hairbrush for comparison with braided hair found by hikers ten years earlier. The analysis suggested a match, though DNA testing wasn't advanced enough yet for definitive identification.

On a clear August morning, geologist Cecilia Travis was carefully examining the terrain when something caught her eye. Partially buried in the rocky soil was a human skull with a distinctive gold tooth.

The dental records confirmed what everyone hoped and feared: They'd found Michelle Wallace.

Over the following hours, the search team meticulously recovered about eighty-five percent of Michelle's skeleton from the forty-degree slope. The condition and distribution of the remains told a grim story—her body had been thrown down the incline from the road above, and scavenging animals had scattered some of the bones over the years.

They also found personal items that confirmed Michelle's identity: fragments of her clothing, her hiking boot with foot bones still inside, and remnants of her backpack. Among the clothing fragments was a zipper from her jeans that had been forcibly ripped from the zipper teeth, leading investigators to believe she had been sexually assaulted. The evidence painted a picture of what had happened after Roy Melanson had convinced her to drive him to this remote location.

While the exact cause of death couldn't be determined due to decomposition, investigators were now certain that Michelle had been murdered and assaulted. And they had a prime suspect sitting in a Kentucky jail, where he'd been serving time for burglary since his 1992 arrest.

———

Roy Melanson was extradited to Colorado to face murder charges for Michelle Wallace's death. At fifty-five years old, he'd spent most of his adult life in and out of prison, but he'd never been held accountable for the murders that investigators believed he'd committed.

The trial began in September 1993, almost nineteen years after Michelle's disappearance. The prosecution presented a compelling circumstantial case: Melanson was the last person seen with Michelle, he'd been caught with her belongings and vehicle, and now her body had been found where he'd likely dumped it.

The defense argued that without a determined cause of death or direct witnesses, reasonable doubt remained. Melanson himself was defiant, even refusing to attend portions of the trial and claiming he was being unfairly persecuted.

His former cellmates provided damaging testimony, describing how Melanson had bragged about killing a young woman and hiding a body in the mountains. The pattern of his other crimes gave context to the violence Michelle had likely endured.

On September 3, 1993, the jury found Roy Melanson guilty of first-degree murder. The judge, clearly disgusted by the defendant's lack of remorse, called him "a waste of humanity" as he handed down a sentence of life in prison without the possibility of parole.

For George Wallace, who'd endured nearly two decades of uncertainty, the verdict brought some measure of closure. His daughter's killer would never see freedom again, and Michelle's remains could finally be laid to rest beside her mother.

———

In 2000, a new federal law required all incarcerated felons to submit DNA samples for inclusion in the national CODIS database. Roy Melanson, now serving his life sentence in Colorado, had no choice but to comply.

The DNA sample sat in the system for years before cold case investigators began using it to solve decades-old crimes. In 2009, the sample hit matches in two separate cases that would finally bring justice for other victims.

Detective Don Winegar in Napa County had never given up on the Anita Andrews case. When the cigarette butt from Fagiani's Cocktail Lounge was tested for DNA, the results were unambiguous: Roy Melanson had been in that bar on the night Anita was murdered.

Additional DNA evidence from a bloody towel at the scene also matched Melanson, providing overwhelming proof that he was Anita's killer. After thirty-seven years, investigators finally had their answer.

Meanwhile, in Louisiana, DNA from semen found on Charlotte Sauerwin's clothing also matched Melanson's profile. The .380 caliber pistol he'd been carrying when arrested in Kentucky was traced back to Charlotte through its serial number, which had been chemically restored despite being filed off.

Suddenly, authorities in multiple states were coordinating arrests and indictments for murders that had gone unsolved for decades.

————

Roy Melanson was eighty-three years old when he died in the Colorado Territorial Correctional Facility on May 22, 2020. He'd spent his final years in a wheelchair, his health deteriorating as he served multiple life sentences for the murders he'd finally been convicted of committing.

The news of his death wasn't made public until 2021, when Napa County officials contacted the prison to check on his status for legal proceedings. By then, Melanson had been dead for nearly a year, taking whatever secrets he still held to his grave.

He'd been convicted for the murders of Michelle Wallace and Anita Andrews, and indicted for Charlotte Sauerwin's death. The Pauline Klumpp case remained officially unsolved, though investigators never doubted Melanson's responsibility for her disappearance.

•

CHAPTER 7

THE GILBERT GOONS

The emergency dispatcher's voice cut through the static at 9:49 p.m. on October 28, 2023. "Respond to 194th Street and Via Del Rancho, Queen Creek. We have a sixteen-year-old male down in the roadway with life-threatening injuries."

The first officer to arrive at the scene swept her headlights across what should have been a quiet residential street in one of Arizona's most affluent suburbs. Instead, she found chaos. Teenagers scattered like startled deer, some still in Halloween costumes. Red and blue party cups littered the asphalt. And there, lying motionless in the middle of the road, was Preston Lord.

The boy's face was swollen beyond recognition. Blood pooled beneath his head, reflecting the spinning emergency lights. A group of panicked teens surrounded him, some attempting CPR while others sobbed uncontrollably. One girl in a vampire costume knelt beside Preston, her hands covered in his blood.

"He was just walking away from the party," she gasped to the officer. "They came out of nowhere."

Preston's breathing was shallow, erratic. Paramedics arrived within minutes and immediately began advanced life support measures. As they loaded him into the ambulance, the officer surveyed the scene. This wasn't a random assault or a simple fight gone wrong. The evidence scattered across the pavement told a different story—one of organized violence that had been building for months in Gilbert's shadow.

———

Gilbert, Arizona, had always been the poster child for American suburban success. With its manicured lawns, championship high school sports teams, and median household income well above the national average, it consistently ranked among the safest cities in the United States. Soccer moms drove luxury SUVs to Target, and teenagers worried more about college applications than street crime.

But beneath the surface of this desert paradise, something had been festering.

Preston Lord was exactly the kind of kid Gilbert was designed to protect. At sixteen, he was a sophomore at Combs High School, a lanky basketball player whose infectious laugh could fill a gymnasium. His stepmother, Autumn, often joked that Preston never met a stranger—he had this gift for making people feel welcome, whether they were new teammates or classmates eating lunch alone. His biological father, Nick, coached his youth basketball teams and watched with pride as his son developed into both a skilled athlete and a young man of character.

On the evening of October 28, Preston had no plans beyond hanging out with friends. It was the Saturday before Halloween, and social media was buzzing about parties across the East Valley. One in particular had caught the attention of teenagers throughout Gilbert, Queen Creek, and the surrounding suburbs: a costume party advertised on Snapchat with promises of free alcohol and minimal adult supervision.

Preston wasn't much of a partier, but his basketball team-mates convinced him to check it out. They'd show up, see what was happening, and maybe stay for an hour. What harm could there be in a quick appearance at a Halloween party in one of Arizona's safest communities?

———

The house on Via Del Rancho belonged to the parents of a teenage girl whose friends had convinced her to throw a party while her parents were out of town. What started as a small gathering quickly spiraled out of control as word spread across social media platforms. By 9:00 p.m., nearly two hundred teenagers had descended on the quiet Queen Creek neighborhood.

Most were typical suburban kids looking for weekend enter-tainment. However, scattered throughout the crowd was a different element entirely—a loose confederation of older teenagers who called themselves the Gilbert Goons.

The Goons weren't a traditional gang in any sense. They had no colors, no formal leadership structure, and no territorial boundaries to defend. Instead, they were something more insidious: affluent teenagers who had bonded over a shared appetite for violence. Their "brand" was chaos, and their weapon of choice was social media.

Treston Billey arrived at the party dressed in a white pinstriped suit, playing the part of a 1920s gangster. At eighteen, he was one of the older attendees, and his presence commanded attention. Billey had been instrumental in organizing many of the Goons' previous "activities"—group assaults that were filmed and shared on Snapchat like entertainment.

Jacob Meisner, seventeen, was part of the core group that had been friends since elementary school. Like many of the Goons, he came from a well-to-do family and had never faced serious consequences for his actions. Taylor Sherman, nineteen, was known for his skill with a camera phone and his willingness to document the group's violence in vivid detail.

Talan Renner, also seventeen, had earned a reputation even among the Goons for his aptitude for escalating conflicts. William "Owen" Hines was already well-known to local police, though his juvenile record had done little to curtail his activities. Finally, Talyn Vigil and Dominic Turner rounded out the core group that had arrived at the party with violence on their minds.

None of the partygoers, including Preston Lord, knew that they were walking into a trap that had been months in the making.

———

The Gilbert Goons had been operating with near-impunity since late 2022. Their methodology was simple but effective: Identify isolated targets, often younger or smaller teenagers, and then overwhelm them with superior numbers while documenting the assault for social media.

The attacks followed a predictable pattern. A minor slight —real or imagined—would trigger retaliation. The Goons would use social media to coordinate their response, often drawing from a network of forty to fifty associates. The actual violence was swift and brutal, designed to inflict maximum damage in minimum time. Victims were typically left with broken bones, concussions, and psychological trauma that lasted far longer than their physical injuries.

But perhaps most disturbing was what happened after the beatings. The Goons treated their violence like content creation, editing videos of their assaults and sharing them across multiple social media platforms. The more views and reactions they received, the more emboldened they became.

The attacks had been escalating throughout 2023, each one more brazen than the last. In August, Tristan Kuehner, a junior at Perry High School, was lured to a Gilbert In-N-Out Burger by associates of the Goons. What followed was a savage beating involving Tyler Freeman and others, with Freeman wielding brass knuckles as the group pummeled their victim. The assault was so severe that Tristan's family eventually moved him overseas for his safety, afraid the Goons would return to finish what they'd started.

Freeman had become one of the most violent members, participating in multiple assaults throughout the year with a viciousness that shocked even hardened investigators. William Hines had been arrested multiple times, but he continued to participate in group violence without meaningful consequences; his juvenile record did nothing to slow his descent into brutality.

By October 2023, the Goons had created a climate of fear among teenagers throughout the East Valley. Victims were reluctant to report assaults, knowing that retaliation was swift and severe. Parents were often unaware of the scope of the violence, dismissing their children's concerns as typical teenage drama.

Law enforcement agencies, meanwhile, struggled to connect the dots. Individual assault reports were filed with different departments across multiple jurisdictions. Without victims specifically mentioning the "Gilbert Goons" name, police failed to recognize the organized nature of the violence.

The Halloween party in Queen Creek would change all that.

———

Preston arrived at the party at around 9:00 p.m. with several teammates from his basketball team. The scene was already chaotic—teenagers in costumes crowded into the house and spilled out onto the front lawn. Music pounded from speakers while underage partygoers openly consumed alcohol.

Preston wasn't particularly interested in drinking or causing trouble. He and his friends walked through the party, observing the scene with the detached curiosity of teenagers who knew they probably shouldn't be there but couldn't resist the spectacle.

It was around 9:30 p.m. when the evening took a dark turn.

A fight had broken out between two groups of teenagers near the back of the house. Preston's friend, a Latino boy wearing a "cholo" costume complete with a long gold chain, pulled out his phone to record the altercation. It was a harmless impulse—the kind of thing teenagers do when they encounter drama at parties.

But Treston Billey saw the recording, and he didn't like it.

Billey, still in his white gangster costume, approached Preston's friend with the aggressive swagger that had become his signature. "Delete that video," he demanded. His tone left no room for negotiation.

Preston's friend, sensing trouble, quickly complied—but the damage was done. Billey had identified targets, and the other Goons were watching.

Recognizing that the situation was deteriorating rapidly, Preston and his group decided to leave. They walked away from the party, heading down the street toward their cars. It was a smart decision that should have kept them safe.

But the Goons weren't finished with them.

———

As Preston and his friends walked down the dark residential street, they heard voices behind them. A group of eight to ten older teenagers, most of them dressed in gangster costumes, had followed them from the party. The Goons were taunting them, singing "Na na na na, hey hey, goodbye" in mocking voices. Some were even skipping as if the whole thing were a game.

Preston's group quickened their pace, but they were outnumbered and outmatched. The Goons had planned this moment, coordinating their movements with the precision of a pack hunting prey.

Suddenly, one of the pursuers reached out and snatched the gold chain from Preston's friend's neck. It was a deliberate provocation, designed to trigger exactly the response it received.

"Run," someone shouted.

Preston and his friends scattered in different directions. One boy managed to hide behind a bush. Another vaulted a fence into someone's backyard. Unfortunately, Preston found himself trapped on a street corner near 194th Street and Via Del Rancho.

The Goons swarmed him like wolves bringing down wounded prey.

———

What happened next lasted only seconds, but those seconds would haunt the Queen Creek community for years to come.

Multiple witnesses later described seeing Preston knocked to the ground by the first blow. According to police reports, Talan Renner allegedly delivered the punch that sent the sixteen-year-old crashing to the asphalt.

But that was only the beginning.

The other Goons formed a circle around Preston's prone body as they began kicking and stomping on him. Their target was his head and torso, and they struck with the calculated precision of attackers who had done this before. Preston tried to protect himself, but he was overwhelmed by the sheer number of assailants.

"He's out!" someone shouted as Preston lost consciousness.

The attackers scattered immediately, running back toward the party and disappearing into the night. Some were reportedly laughing as they fled. A few pulled out their phones to document their handiwork, treating Preston's motionless body like a trophy to be shared on social media.

A neighbor's security camera captured grainy footage of approximately ten figures sprinting away from the scene. By the time horrified partygoers reached Preston, he was alone and unresponsive in the middle of the street.

————

Preston fought for his life for two days at Phoenix Children's Hospital before succumbing to his injuries on October 30th. The Maricopa County Medical Examiner ruled his death a homicide caused by blunt force trauma to the head.

A lead detective from Queen Creek Police had been assigned to what was initially classified as an aggravated assault case. When Preston died, it became the Queen Creek Police Department's first homicide investigation since the department's formation in 2022.

The detective immediately recognized that this wasn't a simple fight between teenagers. The organized nature of the attack, the number of participants, and the severity of Preston's injuries all pointed to something more sinister. Within hours of Preston's death, investigators had learned about the "Gilbert Goons." They began to suspect that the Halloween party assault was part of a much larger pattern.

The investigation would ultimately involve multiple law enforcement agencies across the Phoenix metropolitan area. Search warrants were executed as early as October 31, with investigators focusing on social media accounts, cell phone records, and physical evidence from the scene.

On November 2, police raided Treston Billey's house, seizing his Halloween costume and searching for the stolen gold chain. They also began the painstaking process of interviewing witnesses, many of whom were initially reluctant to cooperate due to fear of retaliation.

The FBI's Phoenix office joined the investigation on November 14, offering a $10,000 reward for information and establishing a dedicated tip line. The federal involvement signaled the seriousness with which law enforcement was treating the case, but it also reflected the challenges they faced in prosecuting affluent teenagers whose families had the resources to mount sophisticated legal defenses.

Perhaps most damaging to the suspects were their own social media posts. Within hours of Preston's attack, the Goons were bragging about their involvement in group chats and private messages. According to police reports, Talan Renner allegedly sent a message around midnight stating,

> "I got in a fight, a big group fight, and killed a kid. I guess I'm just too strong."

Talyn Vigil reportedly sent a Snapchat message reading,

> "I hit a kid and this kid...hit his head and then they kicked his head in the ground then I got word he died so idk."

Taylor Sherman, who had filmed Preston's motionless body, allegedly shared the video in a group chat with the caption "Slumped the fuck out haha."

These digital breadcrumbs would prove crucial as investigators built their case. Modern teenagers live their lives online, and the Goons' compulsion to document and share their violence became their downfall.

But gathering evidence was only part of the challenge facing law enforcement. The other part was overcoming the culture of silence and intimidation that the Goons had cultivated carefully over months of violent activity.

———

Throughout the fall and winter of 2023, investigators worked methodically to build their case. They faced significant obstacles, including witness intimidation and the complex task of coordinating across multiple jurisdictions. The Goons had operated throughout the East Valley, meaning that evidence was scattered across Gilbert, Queen Creek, Mesa, Chandler, and other communities.

Detectives compiled over 2,000 pages of reports and 600 video clips related to the case. They discovered that the Gilbert Goons had been involved in at least eighteen separate violent incidents, with some individual attacks involving multiple victims.

The scope of the investigation grew; authorities realized they weren't just dealing with Preston's murder, but with a systematic campaign of teen violence that had terrorized the East Valley for months.

In December 2023, Gilbert Police reopened four previously shelved assault cases after recognizing their connection to the Goons. Other departments began reviewing their own files, looking for patterns they had previously missed.

By February 2024, investigators had submitted their findings to a grand jury. The evidence was overwhelming—not just for Preston's murder, but for a conspiracy of violence that had operated with impunity in one of America's safest communities.

————

On March 6, 2024, Maricopa County Attorney Rachel Mitchell held a late-night press conference to announce that murder charges had been filed against seven defendants. The next morning, SWAT teams and police units conducted coordinated raids across the East Valley.

The sound of helicopters and police sirens shattered the morning calm in Gilbert's upscale neighborhoods. Neighbors peered through their windows at scenes that looked like military operations—tactical teams in full gear surrounding houses worth millions, officers with rifles drawn as they led teenagers away in handcuffs. The image of wealth and privilege crumbling under the weight of hand-cuffs and orange jumpsuits would haunt the community for years.

By March 7th, all seven defendants were in custody: Treston Billey, Jacob Meisner, Taylor Sherman, Talan Renner, Dominic Turner, William "Owen" Hines, and Talyn Vigil. Each was charged with first-degree murder and kidnapping. Several faced additional charges for aggravated robbery.

The arrests sent shockwaves through a community that had convinced itself such violence could never touch their affluent bubble. Parents who had dismissed concerns about teen violence were forced to confront the reality that their own children might be victims—or even perpetrators.

But the legal battle was just beginning. The defendants' families hired expensive attorneys, and the case would drag on for over a year as prosecutors worked to hold these privileged teenagers accountable for their crimes.

————

In March 2025, William "Owen" Hines became the first to crack under pressure. Faced with the prospect of life in prison and overwhelmed by the evidence against him, he accepted a plea deal that would forever brand him as Preston's killer. Standing before Judge Scott McCoy with his hands shackled, Hines pleaded guilty to manslaughter for Preston's death and admitted to his role in the savage beating.

The plea deal also resolved three other violent cases from his crime spree—two aggravated assaults from 2022 and the drunk-driving crash that had left another victim with permanent brain damage. In total, Hines received seventeen years in prison: twelve years for Preston's manslaughter and five additional years for the DUI assault.

The sentencing hearing was a moment of raw emotion that laid bare the devastating human cost of the Goons' violence. Preston's parents sat in the front row, their faces etched with grief that would never fully heal. His stepmother, Autumn, spoke directly to Hines with words that would haunt the courtroom: "I hope that every day for the rest of your life you remember his name, his face, and the life you cut short."

But Hines' cooperation marked only the beginning of the legal reckoning. The other six defendants chose to fight the charges, confident that their families' wealth and legal resources could save them from accountability.

Jacob Meisner's defiance was particularly striking. At his hearing on May 30, 2025, his attorney announced that Meisner was rejecting all plea offers and would take his chances at trial. The judge's response was chilling: If convicted of first-degree felony murder under Arizona's unforgiving laws, Meisner would face life in prison with the possibility of parole only after twenty-five years. The court-room fell silent as the weight of those words settled over the defendant and his family.

The remaining five defendants—Treston Billey, Talan Renner, Talyn Vigil, Dominic Turner, and Taylor Sherman—also refused to accept responsibility for their actions. The complexity of prosecuting six defendants simultaneously forced multiple delays. Originally scheduled for 2025, their joint trial was pushed back to January 2026 as attorneys on both sides prepared for what promised to be one of Arizona's most closely watched murder trials in recent memory.

Meanwhile, Preston's parents pursued justice through the civil courts. On June 25, 2025, they filed a wrongful death lawsuit against Jacob Meisner's parents, alleging that they knew of their son's violent tendencies yet failed to intervene. The lawsuit cited three prior attacks Meisner had allegedly been involved in, painting a picture of parents who chose willful blindness over difficult conversations about their son's escalating violence.

———

Perhaps the most lasting impact of Preston Lord's death came not from the courtroom but from the state capitol. Lawmakers, horrified by the details of the case, passed "Preston's Law" (House Bill 2611) in mid-2025. The legisla-tion transformed group assaults—commonly known as "swarming" attacks—from misdemeanors into serious Class 4 felonies, ensuring that future perpetrators would face real consequences for mob violence.

Governor Katie Hobbs signed the bill into law as Preston's family watched from the gallery, their son's name now permanently etched into Arizona's criminal code. It was a bittersweet victory—meaningful change born from unbearable loss, a promise that Preston's death would not be in vain.

The Gilbert Goons case exposed uncomfortable truths about privilege, violence, and accountability in modern America. These weren't inner-city gang members fighting over territory or drug profits. They were affluent teenagers who had turned violence into entertainment, confident that their socioeconomic status would protect them from consequences.

For months, they had been right.

Preston Lord's death changed everything. The sixteen-year-old basketball player who had simply wanted to check out a Halloween party became the catalyst for a reckoning that reverberated far beyond Queen Creek's quiet streets.

As of January 2025, five defendants still await trial for first-degree murder, their futures hanging in the balance. Their expensive attorneys continue to file motions and delays, but the evidence against them remains overwhelming. Digital breadcrumbs, witness testimony, and their own bragging messages paint a picture of callous violence that no amount of legal maneuvering can erase.

For Preston's family, no verdict can bring back what was lost on that Halloween night in 2023.

CHAPTER 8

THE FACEBOOK KILLER

The fluorescent lights of the Miami Denny's cast everything in harsh whites and sickly yellows at three in the morning. Jennifer Alfonso moved between tables with practiced efficiency, refilling coffee cups and clearing plates for the late-night crowd of shift workers, insomniacs, and bar refugees looking to sober up over pancakes and hash browns.

At twenty-three, Jennifer had a natural warmth that made customers feel at ease even during the restaurant's graveyard hours. She'd been working nights for months, supporting herself and her young daughter, Isabelle, as a single mother. The tips weren't great, but the work was steady, and her coworkers had become like family.

One customer had started requesting Jennifer specifically whenever he came in. Derek Medina was twenty-eight, average height with a stocky build, and he always seemed to have his phone out, either taking photos or recording videos of himself. He'd order his food, eat slowly, and watch Jennifer work. His tips were generous, his conversation polite but persistent.

"You're different from the other girls here," Derek told her one night, his dark eyes following her movements. "You've got something special."

Jennifer had heard pickup lines before, but Derek's attention felt different—more intense, more focused. He began showing up multiple times a week, always asking for her section, always staying until her shift ended. He told her about his dreams of fame, his writing projects, and his plans for the future. Derek had written several self-published books about spirituality and relationships, and he claimed he'd appeared on television shows as an extra.

Derek's online presence was vast and carefully curated. His Facebook profile overflowed with videos of him boxing, singing karaoke, showing off tattoos, and discussing his paranormal investigations. He described himself as an undefeated professional boxer with a 25-0 record, though he never provided details about specific fights or venues. His social media painted a picture of a man living an exciting, successful life.

"I'm going to be famous someday," Derek told Jennifer during one of their late-night conversations. "I can feel it. People are going to know my name."

———

Derek's pursuit intensified over the weeks. He brought Jennifer small gifts—flowers, coffee, books he'd written. His attention was flattering but overwhelming. He seemed to know her work schedule better than she did, appearing at the restaurant even when she wasn't expecting him.

"You don't need to work these crazy hours," Derek said one night. "A woman like you deserves better than this place."

Jennifer's coworkers noticed Derek's frequent visits and growing familiarity. Some found his devotion romantic; others thought it bordered on obsessive. Derek would sit in Jennifer's section for hours, ordering just enough to justify occupying the table while he watched her serve other customers.

When Jennifer mentioned she was tired from working double shifts, Derek suggested she quit the night job entirely. When she explained she needed the money for Isabelle, Derek offered to help support them both. His generosity seemed genuine, his feelings real.

By late 2009, Derek had worn down Jennifer's resistance. His constant presence had become comfortable and familiar. He made her laugh with his stories about ghost hunting and UFO spotting, he showed her his collection of spiritual books, and he promised a life very different from the world of late-night restaurant work.

In January 2010, Derek Medina and Jennifer Alfonso were married.

———

The honeymoon period was brief. Within months, Derek's charming attention revealed itself as something darker. He questioned Jennifer about her interactions with customers, particularly male ones. He showed up at the restaurant unannounced, claiming he was "checking in" but clearly monitoring her behavior.

Jennifer's boss at Denny's, Amada Cooper, noticed changes in her employee. Jennifer, once outgoing and cheerful, had become quieter and more guarded. Sometimes she arrived at work with bruises on her arms that she explained away as clumsiness.

"Jennifer, you know you can talk to me," Amada said one evening after noticing finger-shaped marks on Jennifer's wrist. "Is everything okay at home?"

Jennifer always deflected such questions with a smile and a change of subject, but her coworkers began to see a pattern. Derek would storm into the restaurant if he thought Jennifer was being too friendly with customers. He'd demand she leave her shift early, causing scenes that embarrassed Jennifer and frustrated management.

Derek's jealousy extended beyond the restaurant. He questioned Jennifer about phone calls, monitored her social media activity, and became angry if she wanted to spend time with friends without him. His need for control manifested in seemingly small ways at first—criticizing her choice of clothes, deciding which movies they'd watch, and insisting she participate in his ghost hunting expeditions.

"He's always got to be the center of attention," one of Jennifer's friends observed. "Even when it's supposed to be about you, somehow it becomes about him."

Derek's online persona grew more grandiose as his real life became more controlling. He posted constantly about his boxing prowess, his television appearances, and his spiritual insights. The contrast between his public image as a successful, confident man and his private behavior as an insecure controller created a cognitive dissonance that Jennifer struggled to understand.

During their separation, Derek's behavior became even more erratic. He began posting angry, vindictive content about Jennifer on Facebook, airing their private disputes for mutual friends to see. The posts were cruel and humiliating, designed to damage Jennifer's reputation and isolate her from their social circle.

———

By early 2012, the marriage had become unbearable. Derek's possessiveness had escalated from emotional manipulation to physical confrontations. Jennifer confided to close friends that Derek had threatened her, though she rarely provided details about specific incidents.

The final straw came during a particularly violent argument. Jennifer's coworkers noticed she'd been absent from work for several days, and when she returned, the bruises on her face couldn't be hidden with makeup.

"That's it," Amada told her. "You need to get out of there before he really hurts you."

This time, Jennifer listened. In February 2012, she filed for divorce.

Derek's reaction was explosive. He bombarded Jennifer with phone calls, showed up at her workplace, and launched a social media campaign against her. He alternated between rage and desperate pleas, promising to change, threatening to hurt himself, and demanding she reconsider.

For several months, Jennifer maintained her resolve. She focused on work, spent time with Isabelle, and began to rebuild her sense of independence. Friends and family watched hopefully as she seemed to rediscover herself outside of Derek's shadow.

———

Derek's campaign to win Jennifer back was relentless. He showed up at the restaurant with elaborate apologies, sent flowers to her home, and enlisted mutual friends to plead his case. He claimed to have sought counseling, to have found religion, to have fundamentally changed.

In March 2012, Derek purchased a townhouse for $107,000 —a gesture he presented as proof of his commitment to providing Jennifer with the stable home life she deserved. The house was in a quiet neighborhood, far from the chaos of their previous living situation.

"I'm a different man now," Derek told Jennifer. "I know I messed up, but I've learned from my mistakes. We can start fresh."

The pressure was intense and constant. Derek seemed to appear everywhere Jennifer went—at the grocery store, at Isabelle's school, at the homes of mutual friends. His persistence was both flattering and exhausting.

Against the advice of friends and coworkers, Jennifer agreed to give the marriage another chance. By summer 2012, she and Isabelle had moved into Derek's new townhouse.

———

The reconciliation brought a temporary period of calm, but old patterns reemerged quickly. Derek's jealousy hadn't diminished during their separation; if anything, it had intensified. He questioned Jennifer more aggressively about her activities during their time apart, demanded detailed accounts of her interactions with other men, and accused her of infidelity without evidence.

Derek's online presence became even more elaborate. He posted videos of himself practicing martial arts, claimed connections to law enforcement through his "neighborhood watch" activities, and continued bragging about his extra work on shows like *Burn Notice*. His need for public validation seemed to grow while his private life became more troubled.

Jennifer's friends noticed as she became increasingly isolated. Derek discouraged her from maintaining friendships, particularly with anyone who had supported her during their separation. He wanted to control not just her activities but her social network, slowly cutting her off from potential sources of support.

The physical violence resumed as well. Jennifer again began arriving at work with bruises, though she'd become more skilled at concealing them and deflecting questions. Her coworkers could see the toll the relationship was taking—the vibrant, confident woman they'd known was disappearing behind a mask of careful compliance.

————

By summer 2013, Jennifer had reached another breaking point. She confided to trusted friends that she was planning to leave Derek permanently this time. The decision terrified those who cared about her—they'd seen Derek's explosive reaction to their previous separation and feared what he might do if pushed too far.

"He's not going to let me go easily," Jennifer told one coworker, "but I can't live like this anymore. Isabelle deserves better."

As the weeks passed, Derek seemed to sense Jennifer's growing distance. His behavior became more erratic, his demands more extreme. He monitored her phone calls, questioned her about conversations with coworkers, and accused her of planning to leave him.

During one particularly heated argument, Derek made his position clear: "You'll never leave me," he told Jennifer. "I'll kill you before I let that happen."

Jennifer had heard threats before, but something in Derek's tone that day convinced her he meant it. She began making discrete preparations—saving money, reaching out to friends who might help her and Isabelle find a safe place to stay, and researching domestic violence resources.

The tension in the house became unbearable. Every conversation was a potential trigger, every interaction fraught with unspoken threats. Derek's paranoia grew as he sensed Jennifer pulling away, while Jennifer's desperation increased as she felt more trapped.

———

The morning of August 8, 2013, began like many others in the Medina household—with tension barely contained beneath a veneer of normalcy. Jennifer had planned what she called a "date night" at home—an early morning movie session together. It was the kind of gesture she hoped might ease the constant friction between them.

When Jennifer overslept and missed their planned start time, she blamed Derek for not waking her. The accusation sparked an argument that quickly escalated beyond its trivial origins. In their upstairs bedroom, around 10:00 a.m., voices rose as frustrations that had been building for months finally exploded.

Derek retrieved his .380-caliber pistol from the upstairs closet and pointed it at Jennifer. The sight of the weapon should have ended the argument, but Jennifer's anger had reached a point where even the threat of violence couldn't stop her.

"Go ahead, call the cops," she told him defiantly.

The confrontation moved through the house as both their tempers spiraled out of control. Security cameras throughout the home captured fragments of their fight— Derek took the gun back upstairs while Jennifer throwing objects in frustration, both of them shouting, the argument spilling from room to room.

In the kitchen, Jennifer grabbed a large knife from the counter. Whether she intended to defend herself or threaten Derek wasn't clear, but Derek was bigger and stronger. He easily wrestled the weapon away and placed it in a drawer, removing Jennifer's only means of protection.

"I'm leaving you," Jennifer announced, the words hanging in the air like a challenge.

Those three words—simple, declarative, final—triggered something in Derek that transformed their domestic dispute into something far more dangerous.

Jennifer began hitting Derek with her fists, striking at his head and temples while he tried to dodge her blows. The physical altercation was brief but intense, fueled by years of accumulated resentment and fear.

Derek made a decision that would define both their futures. He went back upstairs to retrieve his gun a second time.

Derek Medina

When Derek returned to the kitchen, weapon in hand, Jennifer was still there. What happened next lasted only seconds, but it would reverberate across social media and international news.

Derek opened fire on his wife at point-blank range, pulling the trigger repeatedly until the clip was empty. Eight bullets struck Jennifer as she fell to the kitchen floor. The sound of gunshots echoed through the house, followed by a silence that seemed to stretch forever.

Jennifer Alfonso died where she fell, wearing black yoga pants and a black tank top, the kitchen linoleum around her stained with blood. Her arms showed defensive wounds where she had tried desperately to shield herself from the gunfire.

What Derek did next would transform a domestic murder into an international sensation, forever changing how the world viewed the intersection of violence and social media.

Instead of calling 911, instead of checking on ten-year-old Isabelle upstairs, and instead of showing any remorse for what he'd done, Derek pulled out his phone and took a photograph of Jennifer's body.

The image showed Jennifer collapsed backward on the floor, blood visible on her face and arms, her lifeless form a testament to the violence that had just occurred. Derek examined the photo, seemingly satisfied with what he'd captured, and then began composing a message to accompany it.

At 11:11 a.m., Derek uploaded the image to his Facebook profile along with a confession that would shock the internet:

 "I'm going to prison or death sentence for killing my wife. My wife was punching me and I'm not going to stand anymore with the abuse so I did what I did. Hope you understand me. Love you guys, miss you guys, take care Facebook people. You'll see me in the news."

The post appeared instantly in the newsfeeds of Derek's 164 Facebook friends. Many initially thought it must be some kind of sick joke—surely no one would actually photograph their wife's dead body and post it online. But as friends began calling Derek's phone and getting no answer, the horrible reality began to sink in.

Comments appeared under the post within minutes. "Derek what did you do?" wrote one friend. "This can't be real," posted another. While some tried to call Derek directly, others contacted the police, all struggling to process what they were seeing.

Derek posted a second message shortly after the first: "RIP Jennifer Alfonso," accompanied by the same gruesome photograph.

Within an hour, the posts had been shared over 100 times as Derek's friends forwarded the content to family members, news outlets, and anyone who might be able to help. The image of Jennifer's body spread across the internet like a virus, reaching far beyond Derek's immediate circle.

———

After posting his digital confession, Derek changed out of his bloodspattered clothes and began what seemed like a farewell tour. He drove to his parents' house and told his father what he had done, confessing the murder with the same matter-of-fact tone he'd used in his Facebook post.

Derek called his workplace supervisor to report that he had killed his wife and wouldn't be coming to work. He stopped by his aunt's house "to say goodbye," according to family members. Throughout this bizarre series of visits, Derek showed no signs of remorse or panic—only a strange calm, as if he'd completed an unpleasant but necessary task.

Meanwhile, ten-year-old Isabelle remained alone in the house with her mother's body. Derek had told her to stay in her room before leaving, and the frightened child obeyed, unaware of the horror that had occurred downstairs.

The Facebook posts remained online for over five hours, continuing to generate shares and horrified comments. Jennifer's family learned of her death not from police or Derek himself, but from friends who had seen the posts and called them in panic and disbelief.

Just after noon, Derek walked into the South Miami Police Department with his father by his side. He approached the front desk officer and made a statement that shocked officers.

"I just shot my wife," Derek said calmly. "I'll be going to prison."

———

Detective Jonathan Grossman and Detective James Hatzis arrived at the police station to find Derek Medina sitting quietly in an interview room, showing no signs of distress or regret. When they informed him of his rights, Derek waived his right to remain silent and began telling his story.

Over the course of a twenty-six-page statement, Derek described the morning's events in detail. He maintained that Jennifer had been the aggressor, that she had attacked him with both objects and a knife, and that he had acted in self-defense when she began punching him.

"I do not feel that I'm guilty, and I feel like this was self-defense," Derek told the detectives. His affect remained strangely calm throughout the interview, occasionally becoming prideful when describing his actions.

While Derek recounted his version of events, patrol units had rushed to the address on SW 67th Avenue. Officers found the front door unlocked and discovered a scene that matched Derek's Facebook photo exactly. Jennifer's body lay in the kitchen, surrounded by blood, while they found Isabelle hiding in her bedroom upstairs, terrified but physically unharmed.

Officers gently escorted the child from the house, carefully shielding her from the sight of her mother's body. The little girl was taken to relatives while crime scene technicians began the painstaking work of documenting evidence.

———

The physical evidence at the scene began telling a story that contradicted Derek's claims of self-defense. Crime scene investigators found eight shell casings scattered around the kitchen, confirming that Derek had indeed "emptied the clip" as he'd described to detectives.

The .380-caliber pistol was recovered from the house, along with the kitchen knife Derek claimed Jennifer had wielded. The knife was clean and properly stored in a drawer, with no blood or other evidence suggesting it had been used as a weapon.

Investigators documented the trajectory of each bullet wound, noting that all eight shots had been fired from above, suggesting Jennifer was in a low position when killed. The close-range nature of the shots was evident from gunpowder residue found on Jennifer's body and clothing.

Derek's home security system provided crucial footage of the morning's events. While the cameras hadn't captured every moment of the confrontation, they recorded enough to verify some of Derek's claims while contradicting others. The video showed Jennifer throwing objects during their argument and confirmed there had been a physical struggle in the kitchen.

However, the footage also revealed periods when Derek had removed himself from the situation, undercutting his claim that he was in constant danger. Most significantly, the video showed Derek's deliberate trips upstairs to retrieve his weapon—first to threaten Jennifer, then to return for the final, deadly confrontation.

————

Police seized multiple electronic devices from the house— two cell phones, three computers, and an iPad—in their search for any evidence of premeditation or additional communications about the murder. The devices revealed Derek's extensive digital life, including his prolific social media posting and the self-published books he'd written.

Facebook cooperated with the investigation, providing records of Derek's posts and account activity. The timing of the uploads, the metadata associated with the images, and the sequence of Derek's online activity all became part of the evidence file.

The social media company faced criticism for how long the posts had remained online. For over five hours, the grue- some image of Jennifer's body continued to circulate, trau- matizing friends, family, and strangers who encountered it through shares and news coverage. Facebook eventually removed Derek's entire profile and suspended his account.

————

The medical examiner's autopsy provided the most damning evidence against Derek Medina's self-defense claim. Dr. Emma Lew's examination revealed that Jennifer had been shot eight times, with wounds to her torso and arms. All the bullets had followed a downward trajectory, indicating they were fired from above while Jennifer was in a low position.

Gunpowder residue on Jennifer's body confirmed the shots were fired at point-blank range. Most significantly, the examination revealed defensive wounds on Jennifer's arms— clear evidence that she had raised her hands to try to block the gunfire.

The wound patterns were inconsistent with someone actively attacking an armed opponent. Instead, they suggested someone trying desperately to protect themselves while in a vulnerable, possibly kneeling position.

When police photographed Derek days after the shooting, they found only minor bruising on his forearm and a small scratch—hardly the injuries one would expect from the severe beating he claimed to have endured from Jennifer.

———

Within weeks of the murder, a grand jury upgraded the charges against Derek Medina from second-degree to first-degree murder, finding evidence of premeditation in his decision to retrieve the gun a second time after initially removing himself from danger.

Additional charges included child neglect for leaving Isabelle alone with Jennifer's body for several hours, as well as discharging a firearm inside a dwelling.

Prosecutors interviewed Jennifer's coworkers, friends, and family members, building a case around Derek's history of controlling behavior, the forensic evidence, and his callous actions after the fact.

————

Derek Medina's murder trial began in November 2015, more than two years after Jennifer's death. The prosecution opened with a devastating statement: "He didn't just shoot her once. He emptied the clip."

The state's case painted Derek as a controlling, abusive husband whose violence had escalated over time. Jennifer's coworkers testified about bruises they'd seen and Derek's possessive behavior. Her former boss described how Jennifer would arrive at work "bruised up" after violent episodes.

The prosecution presented security footage from the house showing portions of the argument, along with testimony from Detective Grossman about finding Jennifer in a "cowering position" when killed.

Perhaps most powerfully, they called Jennifer's mother, Carolyn Knox, who described learning of her daughter's death by seeing Derek's Facebook post—a testimony that drove home both the brutality of the murder and the cruelty of broadcasting it online.

Derek's defense team faced overwhelming physical evidence. They maintained that he was the victim of an abusive relationship who had reached his breaking point. The defense claimed that Jennifer had been under the influence of drugs on the morning of the murder, pointing to a bottle of alpha-PVP—commonly known as "bath salts"—found in the house as evidence. They also attempted to introduce claims that

Jennifer was a "Satan worshiper," but Judge Colodny ruled both the drug evidence and religious claims inadmissible.

They presented an "expert" witness who claimed to see evidence of Jennifer attacking Derek in reflections visible in security footage—testimony widely viewed as unconvincing.

Derek chose not to testify, leaving his police confession as the primary source of his version of events.

————

After deliberating for six and a half hours, the jury found Derek Medina guilty of second-degree murder on November 25, 2015, rejecting his self-defense claim. While prosecutors had sought a first-degree murder conviction based on premeditation, the jury concluded that Derek had acted in the heat of passion during the domestic dispute rather than with deliberate, premeditated intent to kill. They also convicted him of child neglect and illegally discharging a firearm.

Derek showed no reaction as the verdict was read.

On February 5, 2016, Derek returned to court for sentencing. Jennifer's family addressed the court, with her mother delivering a particularly powerful statement about the permanent loss of her daughter.

Judge Colodny sentenced Derek to life in prison without the possibility of parole for the murder conviction, plus concurrent sentences for the other charges. Before imposing sentence, she referenced Derek's own prophetic Facebook post.

"You foretold your future," Judge Colodny told Derek. "You

wrote on Facebook that 'I am going to prison,' and that is where you will be going."

Derek used his sentencing hearing for a final outburst, proclaiming his innocence and making rambling statements about corruption in the Florida court system. He showed no remorse for Jennifer's death, instead positioning himself as a victim of injustice.

———

Derek Medina appealed his conviction, arguing that evidence about Jennifer's alleged bath salts use should have been admitted and that his expert witness testimony was improperly excluded. However, in 2018, his appeal was denied.

Derek remains in a Florida prison serving his life sentence. His Facebook posts that made him internationally infamous have been removed from the internet, but the case continues to be cited in discussions about domestic violence, social media, and the psychology of murder in the digital age.

For Jennifer Alfonso's family—particularly her daughter, Isabelle—the public nature of the murder compounded their grief and made healing more difficult. The knowledge that strangers around the world had seen Jennifer's final moments became an additional burden they would carry forever.

CHAPTER 9
THE ANIMAL

The phone rang in the Portland Police Bureau just after 6:00 p.m. on July 24, 1979. A young woman's voice, shaking with panic, spoke rapidly to the dispatcher.

"I need help. I came home and found my sister—she's in the bedroom, and she's not moving. I think she's dead."

―――――

Rose Ann Hlavka had just returned from work to the apartment she shared with her twenty-year-old sister, Anna Marie, in northeast Portland, Oregon. The sisters had a routine: Anna worked days at a local business, while Rose worked evenings. They'd pass each other coming and going, sometimes sharing a quick conversation about their plans. Tonight, however, Anna's car sat in its usual spot, and the apartment was eerily quiet.

Rose's heart hammered as she fumbled with her keys, calling Anna's name. No response. The silence felt wrong—thick and suffocating. When she pushed through the unlocked door, everything looked normal at first. Anna's purse sat on the kitchen counter. The television was off. No signs of a struggle in the living room.

But Rose knew something was terribly wrong.

She moved toward the bedroom, each step feeling like walking through quicksand. The door stood partially open. Rose pushed it wider and screamed.

———

The responding officers found a crime scene that would haunt them for decades. Anna Marie's lifeless body lay in her bedroom, the electric cord from her clock radio wound tightly around her neck like a noose. The ligature was embedded so deeply into her flesh that it had nearly disappeared. She had been brutally sexually assaulted before being strangled to death, her body positioned in a way that spoke to her killer's cruelty.

Detective work in 1979 moved at the speed of shoe leather and careful observation. Portland detectives collected what they could from the scene: hair samples, biological evidence, and fingerprints. They knocked on doors throughout the neighborhood, searching for anyone who might have seen a stranger lurking around the apartment complex. They interviewed Anna's coworkers, friends—anyone who might have noticed something unusual in her final days.

But the killer had left no obvious calling card. No witnesses came forward with descriptions of suspicious men. No fingerprints matched anyone in the limited databases available. As summer turned to fall, then winter, the case file grew thicker with dead-end leads and negative laboratory results.

Anna Marie Hlavka's killer had seemingly vanished into thin air.

What the investigators didn't know was that her murderer was already 1,800 miles away, back in Texas, where he had recently been released on parole after serving just five years of a fifteen-year sentence for two counts of rape.

———

Jerry Walter McFadden was a walking nightmare, and the Texas criminal justice system kept setting him free.

Born in Haskell County in 1948, Jerry was a predator almost from adolescence. By age fourteen, he had already dropped out of school and was exhibiting what officials would later describe as "long-standing mental instability and aggressive behavior." His childhood was a breeding ground for violence —dysfunction, poverty, and a complete absence of moral guidance created a monster in human form.

Jerry McFadden

By 1973, at age twenty-five, Jerry had already crossed the line from dangerous to deadly. He pleaded guilty to two horrific crimes: raping a fourteen-year-old girl in Denton and sexually assaulting a high school teacher in Haskell. These weren't crimes of passion or opportunity; they were calculated attacks on vulnerable victims who trusted their community to protect them. The court sentenced him to fifteen years in prison—a sentence that should have meant he wouldn't see freedom until the late 1980s. However, Texas was struggling with massive prison overcrowding in the 1970s, and the state's solution was to hand out "good time" credits like candy on Halloween. Violent predators could cut their sentences nearly in half simply by not causing trouble behind bars.

Jerry McFadden walked out of prison in December 1978, having served just five years. Five years for destroying two lives. Five years for crimes that would scar his victims forever.

He was a free man with unfinished business.

Jerry stood over six feet tall, with wild hair that looked like he'd been electrocuted and a presence that made people instinctively step back. His body was a canvas of violence—tattoos covered his chest and arms, including demonic faces and the words "Death Before Dishonor – The Lonesome Loser" carved into his chest like a manifesto. When fellow inmates eventually nicknamed him "The Animal," they weren't being creative—they were being accurate.

The murder of Anna Marie Hlavka occurred just seven months after Jerry's release from prison, but in 1979, law enforcement agencies operated in isolation. A murder in Oregon had no connection to a paroled rapist in Texas, not in a world without instant communication or computerized databases. Jerry was able to travel state to state like a predator following migration patterns, leaving devastation in his wake without anyone connecting the dots.

He returned to Texas undetected, and by October 1979, he was behind bars again for violating his parole.

The parole violation wasn't a technicality; it was another vicious crime. In June 1979, just weeks before Anna's murder in Portland, Jerry had stalked and kidnapped an eighteen-year-old woman in Shackelford County, Texas. He had forced her into his vehicle at knifepoint, driven her to an isolated area, and brutally raped her. The attack was methodical, calculated, and designed to terrorize. The young woman had survived, but barely—both physically and emotionally.

When she identified Jerry as her attacker, prosecutors threw everything they had at him. In 1981, while already locked up for the parole violation, Jerry was convicted of aggravated robbery and aggravated sexual abuse. The judge handed down another fifteen-year sentence, and this time, officials promised the sentence would stick.

It didn't.

In July 1985, less than five years later, Jerry McFadden walked out of prison again. The same broken system that had failed the first time had failed again, releasing a predator who was becoming more dangerous with each attack. Wood County Sheriff Frank White had objected to Jerry being paroled to East Texas, warning the parole board that authorities in Jerry's home region were more familiar with his patterns and better equipped to monitor him. His protests were overruled, and Jerry was allowed to move to the small community of Hawkins, Texas, to live with his mother and sisters.

By mid-1985, a three-time convicted rapist was living quietly in rural East Texas, and most of the community had no idea.

———

Hawkins was the kind of place where people didn't bother locking their doors. Nestled in Wood County among the piney woods of East Texas, it was a close-knit town where everyone knew their neighbors and serious crime seemed like something that happened in big cities. The town's teenagers spent their summer evenings at Lake Hawkins, a popular spot for swimming and cruising around in pickup trucks.

Suzanne Harrison embodied everything good about small-town life. At eighteen, she was a high school cheerleader known for her church involvement and infectious grin. She worked at a local pharmacy and was beloved by customers and coworkers alike. Her best friend, Gena Turner, was twenty years old and equally accomplished—a former Miss Hawkins High School and valedictorian of the Class of 1984. Gena was attending Tyler Junior College with plans to become a nurse. Both young women represented the best and brightest of their community.

On Sunday evening, May 4, 1986, Suzanne and Gena made plans to meet up with Bryan Boone, a nineteen-year-old recent graduate and athlete also enrolled at Tyler Junior College. The three friends planned to spend the evening riding around Lake Hawkins, enjoying the cool night air at a popular hangout spot called "The Point." It was the kind of innocent recreation that defined teenage life in small-town Texas.

They waved goodbye to their families that evening, expecting to be home by curfew. None of them would ever return.

———

Jerry McFadden had been prowling around Lake Hawkins that Sunday in a blue-and-white Ford Bronco registered to his mother, Dorothy. As evening approached, he had already had one disturbing encounter that would later prove significant.

At around 7:45 p.m., a young couple parked near the lake noticed a wild-haired, tattooed man approaching their vehicle. The stranger asked them for money and then made a crude sexual proposition. When they declined, he pulled a gun on them. The terrified couple managed to talk their way out of the situation—they offered the man a beer and convinced him they had no money. Eventually, he let them go, but not before they got a good look at his disheveled appearance, glimpsed the distinctive tattoo on his chest, and noted that he was standing beside a blue-and-white Bronco. They even managed to catch part of the license plate number.

The couple immediately drove to report the incident to authorities, providing a detailed description of their attacker and his vehicle. They had no way of knowing they had just escaped an encounter with a predator who would soon turn his attention to three other young people at the same lake.

Sometime that evening, Jerry McFadden encountered Suzanne, Gena, and Bryan. Witnesses later recalled seeing the three friends in the company of an unfamiliar, scruffy-looking older man driving a Ford Bronco.

What happened next would terrorize East Texas and spark one of the largest manhunts in the state's history.

———

When Suzanne, Gena, and Bryan failed to return home by their curfew, their families grew alarmed. These were responsible young adults who didn't worry their parents. By late that night, Bryan Boone's brother went out searching for them. He found Bryan's pickup truck abandoned near the lakeshore, about half a mile from where the armed confrontation with the couple had occurred earlier that evening.

Inside the truck, Bryan's brother discovered the purses of both young women, their personal belongings scattered as if they had been forcibly separated from them. There was no sign of the three friends themselves.

At dawn on Monday, May 5, 1986, a community-wide search effort began. Volunteers combed the woods and backroads around Lake Hawkins, while law enforcement organized a systematic grid search. Everyone hoped the three friends had simply gotten lost or had car trouble somewhere in the vast East Texas wilderness.

Those hopes were shattered by the afternoon.

————

A cleanup crew working in a remote area about twenty-five miles north of Lake Hawkins stumbled upon a horrifying discovery. In a ditch off a secluded road, they found the body of eighteen-year-old Suzanne Harrison.

The crime scene was a masterpiece of brutality that would haunt investigators for the rest of their careers. Suzanne Harrison lay in the ditch like discarded garbage, but every detail of her death told a story of prolonged suffering.

She had been beaten so savagely that her face was unrecognizable—what investigators grimly described as "beaten to a pulp." Blood matted her hair and pooled beneath her head where it had struck rocks and hard ground. Her body bore the unmistakable signs of violent sexual assault. Her clothing was torn, defensive wounds covered her hands and forearms, and bruising covered her body, showing the level of her attacker's rage.

But the most chilling detail was how she died. Jerry had strangled her with her own white lace underwear, twisting the delicate fabric into an instrument of death. The ligature was still wrapped around her neck, knotted so tightly that it had cut into her flesh. In her clenched fists, investigators found clumps of grass and thorny weeds—evidence of her final, desperate struggle for life as Jerry McFadden squeezed the breath out of her.

Near Suzanne's body, the search team made another horrifying discovery: articles of Gena Turner's clothing scattered like breadcrumbs along a trail of violence. Shorts and underwear lay crumpled in the dirt, suggesting that Jerry had forced Gena to undress in this same isolated spot. The implication was clear—Gena had been sexually assaulted here too, probably while watching her best friend die.

But where were Gena and Bryan?

———

Word of Suzanne's murder spread quickly through Hawkins, a community unused to such violence. Fear gripped the small town as residents realized that whoever had committed this atrocity might still have two more victims in his control.

Law enforcement agencies mobilized on an unprecedented scale. Wood County Sheriff's deputies, Texas Rangers, and officers from surrounding counties coordinated their efforts. They knew they were racing against time.

The description from the couple who had survived the robbery attempt at the lake proved invaluable. Officers had a solid suspect vehicle and a partial license plate number. They also had a detailed description of the suspect: a wild-haired, tattooed man who had shown the couple a distinctive chest tattoo.

The breakthrough came just two days after the abduction. On May 6, 1986, police spotted a blue-and-white Ford Bronco matching their suspect description near Loop 564 and State Highway 37 north of Mineola in Wood County. Officers pulled the vehicle over and ordered the driver out.

The man behind the wheel was Jerry Walter McFadden. A quick check of his license plate confirmed it matched the prefix given by the lake robbery victims. To remove any doubt, one of the first things deputies did was have Jerry lift his shirt, revealing the "Lonesome Loser" tattoo on his chest exactly as the couple had described.

Jerry was promptly arrested and taken into custody on suspicion of aggravated robbery while investigators worked to link him to Suzanne's murder and the disappearance of Gena and Bryan. He was held at the Wood County Jail on a $100,000 bond as the primary suspect in the unfolding murder case.

———

Evidence against Jerry mounted quickly. David Lee Marsh, who lived near Lake Hawkins, reported seeing Jerry drive past his house on May 4. Gregory Boykin and Levida Pace had been sitting on a porch near the lake and saw Jerry cruise by twice that evening—once around 7:20 p.m. and again about 8:00 p.m. During one pass, they testified, they saw Bryan Boone in the Bronco with Jerry, along with what appeared to be two other people in the truck's cab. They had even waved at Bryan, a familiar face in the community, but noted he didn't wave back—an uncharacteristic behavior that, in hindsight, suggested the young man was under duress.

Forensic evidence also tied Jerry to the crime. Investigators found ammunition in his Bronco that ballistic analysis showed was the same type and caliber as bullets that would later be recovered from victims' bodies. Hair samples taken from Jerry matched hair found on Suzanne's body, and fibers from his clothing matched the fabric of the sweater she had been wearing that night. The evidence painted a picture of prolonged, intimate contact between predator and prey.

Perhaps most damning was information from Jerry's girl-friend, Debbie West. She told investigators that Jerry kept a .38-caliber revolver in her car, but the day after the murders, she noticed the weapon was missing. Debbie provided the police with spent shell casings that Jerry had previously fired from that revolver. Ballistics experts would soon have a chance to compare those casings to bullets recovered from crime scenes.

While Jerry sat in jail maintaining his innocence, the search continued for Gena Turner and Bryan Boone in the woods and backroads of East Texas. Their families and the entire community feared the worst.

————

Five agonizing days after the trio disappeared, searchers made another grim discovery. On Friday, May 9, 1986, the decomposed bodies of Gena Turner and Bryan Boone were found in a rural area about eight miles from where Suzanne had been discovered. Their corpses had been dumped in a ditch off a county road in neighboring Upshur County.

The discovery answered one terrible question while raising another, more urgent one: If Jerry had executed Gena and Bryan in the early morning hours after killing Suzanne, what had he done to them during those long hours in between? The timeline suggested a night of unimaginable terror for the two surviving friends, who had watched their best friend die while knowing they would be next.

Both victims had been shot with a .38-caliber pistol—the same caliber weapon Jerry carried. Bryan had been shot twice, Gena once. The ballistics evidence was overwhelming: Spent shell casings matched those that Jerry's girlfriend had provided to police, confirming that Jerry's missing revolver was the murder weapon.

But the condition of the bodies told a more complex story. Given the advanced state of decomposition after five days in the Texas heat, the medical examiner couldn't determine if Gena had been sexually assaulted before her death. However, the presence of her clothing at Suzanne's murder scene suggested she had endured the same torture as her friend.

Residents near the remote dump site later told investigators they had heard gunshots in the early morning hours of May 5. Two shots, a pause, and then a third shot at around 3:00 a.m., followed minutes later by the sound of a vehicle speeding away. The timeline suggested Jerry had held the victims for hours after killing Suzanne, before finally executing Gena and Bryan in the middle of the night.

Jerry McFadden had driven them roughly forty miles from Lake Hawkins, deeper into an isolated area of Upshur County, where he'd ended their lives with gunfire. The three victims were left scattered across the East Texas countryside like discarded refuse.

The recovery of Gena's and Bryan's bodies brought the toll of Jerry's May 4 crime spree to three homicides—a triple murder that devastated the small town of Hawkins. As news of the additional murders spread, authorities upgraded the charges against Jerry. He was now facing capital murder charges for killing Suzanne Harrison, since her murder was committed in the course of aggravated sexual assault, making it eligible for the death penalty under Texas law.

But even before prosecutors could move forward to trial, Jerry McFadden would unleash another shock on the community.

———

After his arrest in early May 1986, Jerry was transferred to the Upshur County Jail in Gilmer, since two of the victims' bodies had been found in that jurisdiction. He was held there in anticipation of his capital murder trial, but Jerry had no intention of waiting for Texas justice to run its course.

Jerry's escape plan was audacious, violent, and perfectly executed. On July 9, 1986, he asked for permission to make a phone call—a routine request that shouldn't have raised any red flags. Deputy Kenneth Mayfield, a fifty-three-year-old veteran officer, escorted Jerry from his cell to the phone area.

Jerry had spent weeks preparing for this moment. He had secretly loosened a heavy piece of metal from his cell window frame, working on it night after night until it could be pried free. Now, as Mayfield stood beside him, Jerry gripped his improvised weapon and struck.

The metal bar caught Mayfield between the eyes with a massive crack. The deputy dropped like a stone, blood pouring from his head. Jerry didn't stop there—he overpowered a second guard who came running at the sound of the commotion, then locked both injured officers inside empty cells.

With the guards neutralized, Jerry moved through the jail like he owned it. He raided the arms locker, selecting a loaded .38-caliber service revolver and stuffing several hundred dollars in cash from the inmate commissary into his pockets. Then he climbed to the fifth floor of the courthouse building, where the jail's control room housed the communication equipment—and the evening dispatcher.

Twenty-four-year-old Rosalie Williams was alone in the control room when Jerry burst through the door. She looked up from her paperwork to see a wild-haired, tattooed monster pointing a gun at her head. The same hands that had strangled Suzanne Harrison with her own underwear now gripped a loaded revolver, and those cold eyes that had watched three teenagers die were now focused on her.

"Get up," Jerry growled. "You're coming with me."

Rosalie's training kicked in, but there was no protocol for this situation. A suspected triple murderer had just fought his way out of jail and was holding her at gunpoint. She did the only thing she could do—she cooperated and prayed she would live to see morning.

Jerry forced her down to the parking area at gunpoint, where Rosalie's personal vehicle, a sleek Datsun 280ZX sports car, sat in the employee lot. He shoved her into the passenger seat and climbed behind the wheel, and within minutes they were speeding away from Gilmer into the East Texas night.

News of Jerry's escape and armed abduction of a jail employee spread rapidly across East Texas. Law enforcement agencies from multiple counties mobilized immediately. What followed was described as "the biggest manhunt in Texas history," involving hundreds of officers, tracking dogs, helicopters, and roadblocks across the region.

For three days, Jerry managed to elude capture while moving through rural wooded terrain with his hostage. When the stolen car overheated on a back road, he and Rosalie took refuge in an empty railroad boxcar. Jerry kept Rosalie Williams under his control for approximately sixteen hours, during which she feared for her life at every moment.

In a remarkable act of courage and quick thinking, Rosalie eventually managed to escape. While Jerry was distracted searching for water, she crawled out of the boxcar and quietly made her way to a nearby farmhouse, where she called for help.

After Rosalie's escape, Jerry was alone and on the run with over 1,200 officers swarming the countryside searching for him. Heavily armed search teams and tracking dogs canvassed the woods and rural structures. On July 11, 1986, two days after his escape, Jerry was finally cornered in a vacant house's bathroom near Big Sandy, Texas.

Exhausted, dirty, and covered in scratches, Jerry surrendered without a fight when officers discovered him hiding there. The massive dragnet had paid off, ending forty-eight hours of high anxiety for East Texans.

When a police convoy brought the recaptured fugitive back to jail in Gilmer, an estimated three hundred locals lined the streets. The crowd was angry and vocal—one woman's cry of "String him up!" drew cheers from the assembled residents. The public reaction underscored the fury and anguish Jerry had caused: Not only had he murdered three beloved young people, but his escape had terrorized the region anew.

In August 1986, Jerry was convicted of felony escape and armed robbery for the jailbreak and hostage-taking. He received a life imprisonment sentence for those offenses alone, meaning that even apart from the upcoming murder trial, Jerry would never be free again.

———

The trial for the Lake Hawkins murders took place in 1987. Due to pervasive pre-trial publicity and the enraged public sentiment in East Texas, the venue was moved to Bell County in central Texas to ensure a fair jury. Stephen Tokoly, an experienced former Dallas County prosecutor, was appointed by the governor as a special prosecutor for the case, reflecting its high profile and the desire for expert handling of the capital charges.

Jerry was charged specifically with the capital murder of Suzanne Harrison, as that count provided the clearest path to a death sentence. Notably, prosecutors chose not to charge Jerry separately for the murders of Gena Turner and Bryan Boone, partly to streamline the case and avoid multiple trials. They hoped that a conviction and death sentence for Suzanne's murder would effectively deliver justice for all three victims.

The state's case was overwhelming. Eyewitness testimonies, forensic evidence linking Jerry to Suzanne, the recovered ammunition matching the murder weapon, and the circumstances of his arrest painted a damning picture. The jury heard how Jerry—a recently paroled sex offender with multiple prior rape convictions—had abducted the teenagers, brutally raped and strangled Suzanne, then callously shot her two friends.

Jerry didn't take the stand in his own defense and maintained what many described as a cold or emotionless demeanor throughout the trial. His court-appointed defense team attempted to question procedural issues, but they couldn't refute the physical evidence or eyewitness accounts tying Jerry to the crime.

On July 14, 1987, a Bell County jury found Jerry Walter McFadden guilty of capital murder for the rape and murder of Suzanne Harrison. In the penalty phase, it took the jury of six men and six women only about thirty-five minutes to decide on the ultimate punishment.

Jerry Walter McFadden was sentenced to death by lethal injection. He showed no significant reaction when the verdict and sentence were read.

————

Jerry was sent to Texas Death Row at the Ellis Unit, where he pursued the usual appeals available to capital inmates. Over the following years, various courts reviewed his case, but no court found any credible doubt about his guilt or the fairness of his trial.

The court of appeals affirmed his conviction and sentence in 1993, and his federal appeals were rejected in January 1999. With all appeals exhausted, an execution date was finally scheduled.

On October 14, 1999, after twelve years on Death Row, fifty-one-year-old Jerry "The Animal" McFadden was executed by lethal injection at the Huntsville Unit in Texas. He declined to make any final statement before the lethal drugs were administered.

Witnessing the execution were family members of the victims, who had waited thirteen years for this moment of justice. Suzanne Harrison's mother, father, and brother were present. As Jerry was led into the chamber, Suzanne's mother burst into tears and cried out, "He looked at me," then turned away sobbing. After watching Jerry take his last breaths, Suzanne's brother Craig remarked, "He's gutless." He later added, "We settled the bill today... he has paid for it with his life. It was way overdue."

The victims' families expressed relief that Jerry's punishment was finally carried out, though their statements emphasized that no execution could bring back the three young lives he had stolen.

————

The story of Jerry "The Animal" McFadden might have ended there, with his execution in 1999. However, forty years after Anna Marie Hlavka's murder in Portland, Oregon, her case was about to be solved in a way that would have seemed like science fiction to the detectives who first investigated her death.

In 2009, retired detective volunteers in Portland reviewed Anna's cold case, submitting evidence to the Oregon State Police Crime Lab for forensic testing. In 2011, lab technicians made an unusual discovery: They were able to extract a full DNA profile of an unknown male from evidence collected at the crime scene four decades earlier. For a case that old, obtaining such a complete DNA profile was remarkable.

Detective Meredith Hopper of the Portland Cold Case Homicide Detail began actively investigating Anna's case in 2012. Over the following years, eight different suspects were investigated and cleared when their DNA was compared to the unknown profile from the crime scene.

In May 2018, inspired by the recent arrest of the "Golden State Killer" through genetic genealogy, Detectives Hopper and Brendan McGuire contacted Parabon NanoLabs to explore this cutting-edge forensic technique for Anna's case. The Oregon State Police Crime Lab agreed that the DNA evidence met the criteria for genetic genealogy testing.

Parabon's chief genetic genealogist, CeCe Moore, explained the process: Her team uploads suspect DNA to public ancestry databases like GEDmatch, where they can identify potential relatives—usually distant cousins. By building family trees of these DNA matches and working backward, they can reverse-engineer the family tree of the unknown suspect.

In July 2018, Parabon conducted its genetic genealogy analysis on Anna's case DNA, finding eight potentially promising matches consistent with third cousins. In October 2018, they delivered their final report: Jerry Walter McFadden appeared to be the killer, as he was the common link among all the familial matches.

The challenge was that Jerry had been executed in 1999, before DNA databases became standard practice. His DNA profile was never entered into the FBI CODIS database for comparison. Detectives would need to obtain DNA from his surviving family members for confirmation.

In November 2018, Detectives Hopper and McGuire traveled to Texas to interview Jerry's relatives. They learned about his travel patterns, including a trip to the Pacific Northwest in 1979—exactly when Anna Marie Hlavka was murdered. Family members confirmed that an acquaintance had dropped Jerry off in Portland that year.

The detectives obtained DNA samples from Jerry's family members and submitted them for comparison. In January 2019, the Oregon State Police Crime Lab provided confirmatory results: Jerry Walter McFadden was definitively the killer of Anna Marie Hlavka.

On January 31, 2019, Portland detectives announced the resolution of the forty-year-old cold case. For Anna's family, it was a bittersweet moment—finally knowing who had taken their sister's life, but realizing that justice in the conventional sense was impossible, since the killer had been dead for twenty years.

———

The resolution of Anna Marie Hlavka's murder raised troubling questions about Jerry McFadden's true scope of violence. If he had traveled from Texas to Oregon to commit murder in 1979, how many other victims might there be? Law enforcement agencies have since reviewed his timeline and travels to see if he can be linked to additional cold cases.

Jerry's criminal career spanned at least thirteen years, from his first rape convictions in 1973 to his final murders in 1986. During that time, he was paroled twice and violated his parole multiple times, providing him with numerous opportunities to commit crimes across multiple states. Given his pattern of sexual violence and murder, investigators believe there may be other unknown victims.

The case also highlighted critical failures in the criminal justice system of the 1970s and 1980s. Jerry was repeatedly released early from prison despite escalating violent behavior. His first parole in 1978 came after serving only five years of a fifteen-year sentence for two rapes. His second parole in

1985 came after serving less than five years of another fifteen-year sentence for aggravated sexual assault.

Sheriff Frank White's warnings about paroling Jerry to East Texas were ignored, with tragic consequences. The system that was meant to protect society instead repeatedly freed a predator who used each opportunity to commit increasingly serious crimes.

Jerry's case—along with that of fellow serial killer Kenneth McDuff, who was also paroled and went on to commit more murders—led to significant reforms in Texas. The state dramatically toughened its parole laws in the 1990s, expanded its prison capacity, and effectively abolished early release for violent offenders.

In Hawkins, the memory of that terrible summer of 1986 remains vivid decades later. The small community lost some of its best and brightest young people to a killer who never should have been free. While Jerry McFadden paid the ultimate price for his crimes, no punishment could ever restore the lives he destroyed or heal the wounds he inflicted on their families and community.

CHAPTER 10

THE LAST MEAL

The grandfather's hands trembled as he dialed 911. Behind him, the Virginia woods stretched dark and silent, hiding secrets he wished he'd never discovered. His voice cracked as the dispatcher answered.

"Oh, my God. I'm just tripping out. What the fuck did he do?"

The emergency operator tried to calm him, but nothing could prepare anyone for what lay hidden in those four black garbage bags scattered among the underbrush. What had started as a grandfather's concern for his grandson's strange behavior was about to uncover one of Spotsylvania County's most brutal murders.

———

In the fall of 2020, Spotsylvania County seemed like any other Virginia suburb. Strip malls dotted the landscape between subdivisions, and teenagers gathered at McDonald's after school, just like everywhere else in America. Among them were former classmates from Massaponax High School who appeared to be navigating typical young adult struggles —relationships, jobs, and the occasional brush with the law.

Bronwyn Meeks had just turned twenty-one and was already the mother of two young children. She moved through her days with the confidence of someone who believed she could handle whatever life threw at her. Her petite frame and youthful appearance often caught people off guard when they learned about her involvement in the local drug scene. She had been in and out of the legal system for minor offenses, but nothing that seemed particularly alarming in a community where such troubles were unfortunately common.

Her boyfriend, Dominic Samuels, was eighteen and carried himself with the swagger of someone who thought he was invincible. He was the father of one of Bronwyn's children, and together, they had carved out what they saw as a profitable niche in the area's drug trade. Dominic was the muscle when needed, but he deferred to Bronwyn's sharper mind when it came to planning and strategy.

Their friend, Brennan Thomas, lived with his grandfather in a modest house where three generations had learned to coexist. At nineteen, Brennan was quieter than his two friends—more of a follower than a leader. He'd known both Bronwyn and Dominic since their high school days at Massaponax, and he maintained the casual friendship that develops among people who've shared classrooms and teenage experiences. His grandfather often worried about the company Brennan kept, but the old man's concerns seemed like typical generational anxiety.

Twenty miles away in Stafford County, Dylan Dakota Whetzel was building his own life with the steady determination that had always defined him. At twenty, Dylan was someone who looked out for his friends—a trait that made him popular but sometimes put him in difficult situations. He worked construction jobs when he could find them and spent his free time with a tight-knit group that had known each other since middle school.

Dylan's friends described him as loyal to a fault. When someone in his circle was struggling, Dylan was the first to offer help, whether that meant a place to stay, money for gas, or just someone to listen. He had strong opinions about right and wrong, and he wasn't shy about expressing them when he saw people he cared about making dangerous choices.

————

The trouble began in late 2020, when one of Dylan's closest friends nearly died from an overdose. The friend had been buying drugs from Bronwyn's operation, and the near-fatal incident had shaken Dylan deeply. What others might have written off as an unfortunate accident, Dylan saw as a preventable tragedy.

He spent days at the hospital, watching his friend fight for their life in the ICU. The doctors weren't sure if there would be permanent brain damage. Dylan's friend's family was devastated, alternating between grief and rage as they tried to understand how someone so young could come so close to death.

For Dylan, the path forward was clear. He needed to confront the person who had sold those drugs.

————

Bronwyn was surprised when Dylan approached her. They knew each other peripherally through mutual friends, but they moved in different circles. When Dylan demanded that she stop selling to his friend, Bronwyn's initial reaction was dismissive. She saw Dylan as naive, someone who didn't understand how the world really worked.

But Dylan was persistent. He showed up at places where he knew Bronwyn would be, always with the same message: Stop selling to his friend, or there would be consequences. He never specified what those consequences might be, but his determination was clear.

For Bronwyn, the confrontation came at the worst possible time. She was facing a court-ordered drug test that she knew she would fail. The walls were closing in on multiple fronts, and now someone was trying to interfere with her business. In a text message to a friend, she revealed a chilling mindset: If she was going back to jail, she wanted to "make it worth her while."

But Bronwyn was calculating. She didn't react with immediate violence or angry confrontation. Instead, she began to plan.

———

By early January 2021, Bronwyn had decided that Dylan represented a threat that needed to be eliminated permanently. She shared her thoughts with Dominic, who was initially skeptical. Selling drugs was one thing, but murder was an entirely different level of criminal activity.

Bronwyn Meeks

Bronwyn was persuasive. She painted Dylan as someone who could bring down their entire operation. If he was willing to confront her publicly about one customer, what would stop him from going to the police about everything else? She reminded Dominic that they had a child together—a family to protect. Sometimes, she argued, violence was the only solution.

Dominic's resistance crumbled as Bronwyn outlined her plan. She wouldn't confront Dylan directly or give him any reason to suspect danger. Instead, she would lure him out under false pretenses. Somewhere isolated, where they could handle the situation without witnesses.

Brennan Thomas was brought into the conspiracy almost by accident. He was at Bronwyn's apartment when she and Dominic were discussing their plan, and his presence made him a liability. Rather than risk him becoming a loose end, Bronwyn decided to make him a participant. She appealed to his loyalty to their friendship and painted the murder as a necessary defense of their shared interests.

The plan took days to develop. Bronwyn studied Dylan's habits, learning where he went and who he spent time with. She identified the best way to approach him without arousing suspicion. Most importantly, she chose the location where they would take him.

The remote intersection of Pamunkey Road and Finney Road behind Brennan Thomas's grandfather's house was perfect for their purposes. Dense woods stretched in all directions, and at night, there was virtually no traffic. It was far enough from Dylan's usual haunts that no one would think to look for him there, but accessible enough that they could get him there without too much difficulty.

———

On January 30, 2021, Bronwyn made her move. She reached out to Dylan with what seemed like an olive branch—an invitation to go out drinking and attend a party. To Dylan, it probably seemed like a chance to smooth things over with someone from his extended social circle.

Bronwyn was careful in how she presented the invitation. She mentioned mutual friends who would be there, places Dylan would recognize, and activities that sounded appealing to a twenty-year-old looking for a good time on a Saturday night. She never directly apologized for their previous confrontations, but her tone suggested that she wanted to put their differences behind them.

Dylan accepted the invitation. Perhaps he saw it as an opportunity to continue his campaign to protect his friend, or maybe he genuinely believed that Bronwyn was ready to make peace. Either way, he agreed to let her pick him up that evening.

When Bronwyn arrived in North Stafford, she wasn't alone. Dominic was in the passenger seat, and Brennan was in the back. Their presence might have given Dylan pause, but these were people he knew. Former classmates who had invited him out for what promised to be a fun night.

The group's first stop was McDonald's. They sat together in the brightly lit restaurant, ordering food and eating like any group of friends on a night out. Dylan chatted easily with the others, perhaps relieved that the evening was starting on such a normal note.

Bronwyn watched Dylan eat his meal with dark satisfaction. In text messages she would send later, she would refer to this dinner as his "last meal"—a reference to the final meal given to condemned prisoners before execution. Even as she laughed at Dylan's jokes and contributed to the casual conversation, she was thinking about what would happen next.

After leaving McDonald's, the group headed toward Spotsylvania County. Bronwyn told Dylan they were going to another friend's house, continuing the party atmosphere. She was deliberately vague about the details, but Dylan didn't press for specifics. He was enjoying himself, probably looking forward to whatever would come next.

As they drove west, the landscape became increasingly rural. Suburban developments gave way to farmland and forest.

The roads grew narrower and darker. If Dylan noticed the isolation, he didn't comment on it.

———

Somewhere during the drive, the atmosphere in the car began to change. Bronwyn started bringing up their previous confrontations, rehashing old grievances. Dylan found himself defending his actions, explaining why he had felt compelled to protect his friend.

The conversation grew more heated. Dominic, who had been largely silent, began to participate, taking Bronwyn's side in the argument. Dylan realized that this wasn't the peace offering he had thought it was.

When Bronwyn suggested they stop the car to "settle things" between Dylan and Dominic, Dylan agreed. He was confident in his ability to handle himself in a fight, and he still didn't fully grasp the danger he was in.

They pulled over in a relatively populated area of Stafford County. Dylan and Dominic got out of the car and began to fight. It was a brief, intense altercation that drew the attention of nearby residents. When it ended, however, instead of going their separate ways, the group convinced Dylan to get back in the car.

Bronwyn played the role of peacemaker, suggesting they continue to the party to cool down and enjoy the rest of the evening. Dylan, perhaps not wanting to seem like he was running away from a fight, agreed to continue with them.

This decision sealed his fate.

Rather than heading to any party, Bronwyn drove them deeper into Spotsylvania County, toward the remote location she had chosen weeks earlier. Dylan began to ask questions about where they were going, but Bronwyn deflected with vague answers about picking up other friends or making a quick stop.

By the time Dylan realized he was being taken somewhere isolated against his will, it was too late to escape.

————

The remote intersection of Pamunkey Road and Finney Road in western Spotsylvania County was exactly what Bronwyn had been looking for. Dense woods stretched in all directions, and at midnight on January 31, there was no one around to hear what happened next.

Bronwyn stopped the car and ordered everyone out. Dylan's confusion turned to alarm as he realized how far they were from civilization. He began to back away from the vehicle, finally understanding that he was in real danger.

The three conspirators moved quickly to surround him. Dylan was outnumbered and far from help, but he didn't give up without a fight. He tried to run into the woods, hoping to use the darkness and his knowledge of the outdoors to escape.

But Dominic and Brennan were prepared for this possibility. They caught Dylan before he could get far from the car. A struggle ensued in the darkness, with Dylan fighting desperately for his life.

The attack was swift and brutal. Multiple gunshots rang out in the darkness—at least six bullets were fired into Dylan's body from behind as he tried to flee. He fell among the trees, his life bleeding away onto the Virginia soil.

In those final moments, Dylan must have understood the complete scope of the betrayal. The people he had trusted enough to get into a car with, the former classmates who had shared a meal with him just hours earlier, had lured him to his death with elaborate lies and false friendship.

But even death wasn't enough to satisfy their twisted plan.

————

Killing Dylan had been only the beginning of what Bronwyn had envisioned. She had always been the planner in her relationship with Dominic, the one who thought through consequences and contingencies. She knew that simply leaving Dylan's body in the woods would eventually lead investigators back to them.

The three conspirators left Dylan's body where it had fallen and drove back to civilization. Over the next day, they went about their normal routines, but Bronwyn was already planning the next phase of their cover-up.

On February 1, Dominic and Brennan made a trip to a local Walmart. Surveillance cameras captured them purchasing a Kobalt axe, paying cash, and avoiding any conversation with the clerk that might make them memorable. They told no one what they intended to do with their purchase.

That evening, they returned to the woods with their new tool. What they did next defied comprehension and revealed the true depths of their callousness.

Using the axe, they dismembered Dylan's body, cutting his remains into pieces that could be more easily concealed. The work was gruesome and difficult, requiring them to return multiple times to complete their grisly task. They showed no remorse as they reduced Dylan from a young man with hopes and dreams to anonymous remains that could be hidden away.

They stuffed the body parts into four large black garbage bags, the kind used for yard waste. The bags were heavy and awkward to carry, leaving trails in the dirt as they dragged them deeper into the underbrush. They scattered the bags in different locations, hoping that even if one was found, the others might remain hidden.

The bloodied axe was left at the scene, abandoned among the trees like evidence of some nightmare that they hoped would never come to light.

———

Dominic and Brennan thought they had been careful, but they had made a critical error. Brennan's grandfather had always been observant, and he had noticed his grandson's increasingly strange behavior over the past few days.

On the night of February 1, the old man saw Brennan and another young man emerging from the woods behind his property. Their clothes were dirty, and they were acting nervous and secretive. When the grandfather asked what they had been doing, Brennan's explanation didn't make sense.

Something about their demeanor had alarmed the older man. He'd raised Brennan since he was a child, and he could tell when his grandson was lying. The more he thought about it, the more convinced he became that something terrible had happened in those woods.

Unable to sleep, the grandfather decided to investigate for himself. He took a flashlight and walked into the woods, following the path he had seen the two young men take earlier.

What he found in the darkness was beyond his worst nightmares.

The black garbage bags were scattered among the trees, some already torn open by animals. The contents were unmistakably human remains, and the bloody axe lying nearby made it clear that this was no accident.

The grandfather's world collapsed in that moment. His grandson, the boy he had raised and loved, was involved in something unspeakably evil.

————

The 911 call came in at 10:00 p.m. on February 1, 2021. The grandfather's voice was filled with shock and disbelief as he tried to explain what he had discovered to the emergency dispatcher.

The operator tried to get more information, but the old man was struggling to process what he had seen. He kept repeating that his grandson had confessed to killing someone, that there were body parts in the woods, that everything had gone terribly wrong.

Spotsylvania County Sheriff's deputies responded immediately, their patrol cars racing through the dark country roads toward the remote location. When they arrived, they found the grandfather waiting by the road, his face pale and his hands still shaking.

The crime scene was unlike anything the responding officers had encountered. The dismembered remains were scattered across a wide area, making it difficult to determine exactly what had happened. The bloody axe provided one clue, but the full scope of the violence would only become clear as investigators processed the evidence.

The remains were quickly identified as those of Dylan Whetzel, the twenty-year-old from Stafford who had been reported missing by concerned family and friends earlier that day.

———

Major Troy Skebo of the Spotsylvania County Sheriff's Office took charge of what was clearly a complex homicide investigation. The brutality of the crime—the multiple gunshot wounds, the dismemberment, the attempted concealment—suggested this wasn't a random act of violence or a crime of passion.

Detectives began the painstaking work of processing the crime scene. They collected the garbage bags and their contents, photographed everything in detail, and searched for any additional evidence that might have been left behind. The axe was bagged as evidence, and investigators began the process of tracing its purchase.

The grandfather's information about Brennan's involvement gave investigators their first lead, but they knew that the scope of the crime suggested multiple participants. The physical evidence supported this theory—there was simply too much work involved in the murder and dismemberment for one person to have accomplished alone.

Detectives began tracking Dylan's movements in his final days, interviewing friends and family members to understand who he had been in contact with. They learned about his confrontation with Bronwyn over the drug sales, and her name quickly moved to the top of their suspect list.

Witnesses reported seeing a Ford Mustang in the area around the time of the murder. Detectives traced the vehicle back to the suspects within hours, finding evidence inside that linked it directly to the crime scene.

————

On February 2, just one day after the body was discovered, investigators arrested nineteen-year-old Brennan Thomas on charges related to the defilement and concealment of a dead body. Thomas was held without bond at Rappahannock Regional Jail, but he refused to cooperate with investigators or provide information about his accomplices.

For several days, detectives worked to identify the other participants in the crime. They initially arrested an eighteen-year-old named Dominic McCall, believing he was the second person seen with Brennan in the woods. But as forensic evidence came in—DNA analysis, fingerprint comparisons, and cell phone data—it became clear that McCall was innocent.

The charges against McCall were dropped, and investigators refocused their efforts on the real perpetrators. Phone records and surveillance footage were providing them with a clearer picture of who had been involved in Dylan's murder.

On February 10, eight days after the discovery of the body, detectives made their move. They arrested Bronwyn Meeks and Dominic Samuels at their respective homes, catching both suspects off guard.

Bronwyn tried to maintain her innocence, but investigators had recovered text messages between her and Dominic that revealed their involvement in the crime. The messages painted a picture of two people who had planned and executed a murder with chilling calculation.

All three suspects were held without bond while prosecutors reviewed the evidence and prepared additional charges. The community was assured that more serious charges, including murder charges, would be forthcoming as the investigation continued.

––––––––

The investigation revealed a web of digital evidence that painted a clear picture of premeditation and extreme brutality. Text messages between the conspirators provided damning insights into their mindsets both before and after the murder.

In one exchange after the killing, Dominic had written to Bronwyn:

> I'm a fucking psychopath and you just saw it firsthand.

The message revealed not remorse but a disturbing pride in his capacity for violence.

Bronwyn, meanwhile, expressed panic about their sloppy execution of the cover-up:

> We're fucked because everything was done so fucking wrong.

Her concern wasn't for their victim, but for their own exposure.

Surveillance footage from the Walmart where the axe was purchased provided additional evidence of premeditation. The video showed Dominic and Brennan selecting the tool, paying cash, and leaving without speaking to anyone who might remember them later.

Cell phone records placed all three suspects in the area where Dylan's body was found, at the time investigators believed the murder had occurred. The digital trail was comprehensive and damning.

The case took on additional complexity when investigators discovered that Bronwyn's mother worked in the Spotsylvania Sheriff's detective division. To avoid any appearance of impropriety or conflict of interest, a special prosecutor, David Sands, was brought in from outside the county to handle the case.

On June 24, 2021, a grand jury returned sweeping indict-ments against all three defendants. Each was charged with first-degree murder and more than eighty other felonies, including murder by mob, abduction, and multiple firearm offenses. The breadth of the charges reflected both the premeditated nature of the crime and the multiple laws broken during its execution and cover-up.

———

As the case moved toward trial, Bronwyn made a calculation that would determine the fate of all three defendants. Facing overwhelming evidence and the possibility of life in prison, she decided to cooperate with prosecutors in exchange for a reduced sentence.

On February 4, 2022, nearly a year after the murder, Bronwyn appeared in court and pleaded guilty to more than thirty felony charges. Her testimony would prove crucial in securing convictions against Dominic and Brennan.

The trials revealed the full scope of the conspiracy and the calculated cruelty involved in Dylan's murder. Brennan was convicted on August 31, 2023, receiving a sentence of life in prison plus eighty-three years. Dominic followed in November 2023, also receiving a life sentence.

In June 2024, Bronwyn was sentenced to forty-two years in prison. At twenty-four years old, she would be in her sixties before she could potentially be released.

Dylan Whetzel's life had been cut short by people he had trusted—young adults who had chosen murder over any reasonable resolution to their conflict. The case would be remembered not just for its brutality, but for the cold calculation behind it: the "last meal" shared with their intended victim, the careful planning, and the complete absence of remorse until they were caught.

In the end, three young lives were destroyed along with Dylan's, though through their own choices rather than the betrayal he experienced. The woods off Pamunkey and Finney Roads returned to their quiet isolation, but they would forever be marked by the violence that had occurred there on that cold January night.

CHAPTER 11

THE BASELINE KILLER

The silver handgun gleamed in the dim light as the man approached three teenagers walking home from church. It was August 6, 2005, and the Arizona heat still radiated from the pavement even as the evening shadows stretched across Baseline Road in Phoenix. The two girls, thirteen and twelve, walked alongside their friend, a boy of a similar age, their conversation light and carefree until the stranger's voice cut through the summer air.

"I just robbed a bank," he said calmly, almost conversationally. "I'm waiting for someone to pick me up."

The children froze. The man's demeanor was eerily composed as he gestured with the weapon toward the darkness behind the church building. None of them dared to run. None of them screamed. They simply followed his commands, walking into the shadows where no one could see them.

In that secluded area, away from street lights and witnesses, the man systematically destroyed their innocence. He sexually assaulted both girls while forcing the boy to watch, his movements deliberate and practiced. When he finished, he pulled out a towel and methodically wiped their bodies, erasing evidence with the precision of someone who understood exactly what he was doing.

Then he vanished into the night, leaving three traumatized children to stumble home in the darkness.

The Phoenix Police Department received the report the next morning. Three juveniles, sexually assaulted by an unknown gunman near Baseline Road. The detective who took the case had no way of knowing he was looking at the first documented attack in what would become one of the most terrifying crime sprees in Arizona history.

Eight days later, the nightmare continued.

———

A woman sat in her car outside a charity donation bin on Thomas Road, placing items in the container under the glow of a parking lot light. She never saw him coming. The man appeared at her passenger window with his silver handgun pressed against the glass.

"Get out," he said.

She obeyed, her hands shaking as she stepped into the humid night air. He slid into the driver's seat and ordered her into the passenger side. The engine started, and they drove through Phoenix streets while he spun the same story about robbing a business and needing a ride to meet his accomplices.

When he found a sufficiently isolated spot, he stopped the

car and turned toward her with cold eyes. "Take off your clothes."

The sexual assault that followed was brutal and methodical. Afterward, he forced her to clean herself with her own clothing, eliminating every trace of physical evidence. When he finally let her go, she was left with nothing but the memory of his voice and the terrifying way he had destroyed her sense of safety.

Two attacks in eight days, both involving the same silver handgun. Both executed with the same chilling precision.

Detective Alex Femenia stared at the reports on his desk, a growing unease settling in his stomach. Phoenix was a large city with its share of violent crime, but these incidents shared disturbing similarities that made him uncomfortable.

———

On September 8, Georgia Thompson fumbled with her car keys in the parking lot of her Tempe apartment complex. It was just after 1:00 a.m., and the nineteen-year-old was exhausted after just finishing her shift, ready to collapse into bed. She never heard the footsteps approaching from behind.

"Leave me alone!" Her voice echoed off the apartment buildings, desperate and terrified.

The gunshot that followed was heard by several neighbors, but by the time anyone looked outside, the parking lot had fallen silent. They found Georgia lying beside her car, keys still clutched in her hand. A single bullet to the head had ended her life instantly.

Her purse sat untouched on the ground beside her. Her wallet contained cash and credit cards, nothing taken.

Whatever had caught the attention of her killer, robbery wasn't the primary motive.

Detectives arrived at the scene and immediately noticed the execution-style nature of the killing. Close range. Single shot to the head. No sign of sexual assault, no evidence of robbery. It was as if someone had walked up to Georgia Thompson and murdered her for the simple reason that they could.

The investigation that followed turned up few leads. Georgia worked as an exotic dancer, which opened several lines of inquiry about disgruntled customers or workplace conflicts. However, interviews with coworkers and regular clients yielded nothing substantial. The case grew cold quickly, filed away as another unsolved homicide in a city that saw too many of them.

Detectives had no way of knowing that Georgia's murder was connected to the sexual assaults happening across town. The killer was escalating, and Phoenix was about to learn the true meaning of terror.

———

The two sisters walked home from the Phoenix city park on September 20, their evening stroll interrupted by the sound of footsteps behind them. The older sister, visibly pregnant, instinctively placed a protective hand over her belly when she turned and saw the man following them. He carried the same silver handgun.

"Don't look at my face," he commanded, forcing them into nearby bushes where the streetlights couldn't reach. "Don't try to see who I am."

What happened next was an exercise in calculated brutality. He raped the younger sister at gunpoint while pressing the barrel of his weapon against her older sister's stomach, threatening to shoot the unborn child if she resisted or tried to run.

The attack wasn't just about sexual gratification—it was about complete domination. He controlled every aspect of their experience, from where they looked to how they positioned their bodies. When he finished the assault, he rubbed dirt on the younger sister's skin, explaining in a matter-of-fact voice that he was eliminating his saliva to prevent DNA identification.

The sisters survived, but the trauma ran deeper than physical injuries. They had been hunted, caught, and violated by someone who understood exactly how to avoid leaving evidence. Someone who had clearly done this before.

Investigators collected DNA samples from the scene, carefully swabbing areas where the attacker might have left biological evidence. The samples went to the Phoenix police lab for analysis, where they joined a growing backlog of evidence from similar cases.

No one realized that those samples contained the key to stopping a killer who was just getting started.

———

September 28 brought a new level of audacity to the crimes.

The three women working the evening shift at the Mexican restaurant near Baseline Road were preparing to close when a figure appeared at the take-out window. The silver handgun emerged from the darkness, pointing directly at the cashier's face.

"Give me the money," he said.

The women scattered, fleeing through the back door into the parking lot, where they screamed for help. The gunman reached through the window, grabbing what cash he could before disappearing into the night.

But he wasn't finished.

Margie was loading groceries into her car with her twelve-year-old daughter, Bianca, when the man materialized beside their vehicle. The same silver weapon, the same calm demeanor, the same impossible choice between compliance and death.

"I just got robbed," he told them, sliding into the backseat. "My friend left me behind. I need you to drive me to meet him."

Margie's hands shook as she started the engine. In the rearview mirror, she could see her daughter's terrified face as the gunman began touching her, his hands roaming over her small body while he directed Margie through Phoenix streets.

"Don't look at me," he warned. "Keep your eyes on the road."

The drive lasted an eternity. When he finally ordered Margie to stop behind an abandoned store, he forced both mother and daughter from the car. In the darkness of that empty parking lot, he raped Margie while her child watched, help-less and terrified.

Afterward, he used their own clothing to wipe down every surface he had touched inside the vehicle. Before leaving, he placed the purse he had stolen from the restaurant into Margie's car, a calling card that would eventually help police connect the crimes. Mother and daughter survived, but their lives were forever changed.

———

November brought bold daylight attacks that demonstrated the killer's growing confidence.

The convenience store clerk on 32nd Street noticed the customer the moment he walked through the door. The dreadlock wig looked obviously fake, and the Halloween mask covered most of his face, but it was the silver handgun that commanded her complete attention.

"Empty the register," he said, his voice muffled by the disguise.

Teresa handed over the cash with trembling fingers, watching as he stuffed the bills into his jacket pocket. He backed toward the door, weapon still trained on her, then disappeared into the night.

Minutes later, across the street, Annelie was placing donations into a charity bin when she heard footsteps approaching. She turned to see a man in a dreadlock wig pointing a silver handgun at her chest.

"I just robbed a store," he said. "I need a ride."

The pattern was becoming his signature—a robbery followed immediately by a sexual assault, with the victim forced to provide transportation between crimes. Annelie found herself pushed into her own car, the gunman sliding into the passenger seat as he directed her to drive through quiet neighborhoods.

When he found a secluded area, he ordered her to remove her clothes. The sexual assault that followed was methodical and degrading, designed to strip away every shred of dignity and control. Afterward, he forced her to spit into her hand and use her own saliva to wipe down areas of her body he had touched.

"No DNA," he explained casually, as if teaching her a lesson in forensic science.

The clinical nature of his evidence destruction was almost more terrifying than the assault itself. This wasn't a crime of passion or opportunity—it was the work of someone who had studied police procedures and knew exactly how to avoid detection.

Four days later, he struck three businesses in rapid succession during a single evening. Las Brasas restaurant, Little Caesar's Pizza, and an attempted robbery of a family in a parking lot. When bystanders tried to intervene, he fired warning shots into the air, then aimed directly at his pursuers as he escaped on foot.

The message was clear: Anyone who tried to stop him would die.

———

Tina Washington stepped out of the restaurant after her workplace holiday party, car keys in hand and a smile on her face. The thirty-nine-year-old preschool teacher had enjoyed the evening with her coworkers, celebrating another successful year of helping children learn and grow.

She never made it to her car.

Peter Ochoa was cleaning up his work area behind the fast-food restaurant when he heard what sounded like fire-crackers popping in the alley. He walked toward the noise, curious about the source, and found a scene that would haunt him for the rest of his life.

A man stood over a woman's body with a silver handgun in his hand. Blood pooled around the victim's head, dark and thick in the parking lot lights. The woman lay motionless beneath him.

The gunman looked up and saw Peter watching. Their eyes met across the alley, and for a frozen moment, neither man moved. Then the killer raised his weapon and pointed it directly at Peter's chest. The trigger clicked, but nothing happened.

The gun had misfired, giving Peter the split second he needed to turn and run. He sprinted toward the street, expecting to feel a bullet tear through his back at any moment, but the shot never came. Behind him, he heard the sound of running footsteps heading in the opposite direction.

When police arrived, they found Tina Washington lying in a pool of blood, shot twice in the head at close range. Her purse was missing, along with a distinctive gold ring inscribed "We love Mom"—a gift from her three sons.

———

Investigators examined Tina's body, noting details that would become sickeningly familiar in the months ahead. Her bra was undone and her pants pulled down slightly, even though there was no evidence of sexual assault. The killer was leaving his signature, a calling card that marked his territory like an animal.

The investigation that followed was massive but largely fruitless. Hundreds of tips poured in from terrified residents, but none led to solid suspects. The composite sketch based on survivor descriptions showed a light-skinned African American man in his forties, but that description could fit thousands of Phoenix residents.

Danny Hamilton, the Phoenix Police Department's ballistics expert, examined the shell casings found at the scene. The .380 caliber rounds would eventually prove crucial to solving the case, but for now, they were just another piece of evidence in a growing pile of clues that seemed to lead nowhere.

———

The murders came in waves after that, each one more brutal than the last.

On February 20, 2006, two women were operating a mobile food truck near 91st Avenue when they were found shot to death inside their vehicle. Romelia Vargas and Mirna Palma-Roman had been preparing breakfast burritos when their killer had struck. Both women lay side by side on the floor of the truck, each killed by a single gunshot to the head. The cash box was empty, and one victim's identification was missing.

The remote location and circumstances initially led police to suspect drug-related violence. The victims were Hispanic women working in an area known for illegal activity, and the execution-style killings suggested organized crime involvement. Detectives spent weeks pursuing leads in the drug trade, interviewing dealers and checking with informants, but they found no connections to the victims.

On March 15, Liliana Sanchez-Cabrera and Chao Chou left work together at around 9:00 p.m., planning to grab dinner before Chao gave Liliana a ride home. They never arrived at either destination.

Police found Liliana's body in the front passenger seat of Chao's abandoned car, partially unclothed and shot in the head. The positioning of her body and her state of undress suggested sexual assault had occurred before the murder. Chao's body was discovered a mile away in an alley. He had been shot in the head.

The killer had forced his way into their vehicle, probably in the restaurant parking lot, then directed Chao to drive to a secluded location. After assaulting Liliana, he executed both victims to eliminate witnesses. The close-range headshots were becoming his trademark—efficient, brutal, and final.

Then, on March 29, a business owner noticed bloody drag marks in his parking lot leading toward storage sheds. Police collected blood evidence but found no victim, leading them to believe someone had been injured in a fight that had moved elsewhere.

Five days later, the overwhelming stench of decomposition led to the discovery of twenty-six-year-old Kristin Nicole Gibbons. Her body, mostly nude and badly decomposed, had been hidden under debris in a storage area. She had been shot in the head and showed signs of a violent struggle— bruises and scratches on her arms and legs indicated she had fought for her life.

The killer had spent time with this victim, perhaps keeping her alive for hours or even days before finally ending her suffering. The level of decomposition made it impossible to determine exactly when she had died, but the brutality of her murder matched the escalating pattern of violence.

———

The eight-year-old boy walked through the front door of his Phoenix home after school, calling out for his mother as he dropped his backpack by the entrance. The house felt wrong somehow—too quiet, too still. He found her in the bathroom.

Sophia Nunez floated face-down in a bathtub filled with bloody water, her dark hair spreading like seaweed around her head. The thirty-seven-year-old mother had been shot in the face at close range, the bullet destroying her features and turning the bathwater crimson.

The boy, moving with the shocked determination of a child who doesn't yet fully understand the permanence of death, turned off the faucet and tried to pull his mother from the tub. When that failed, he attempted CPR, pressing his small hands against her chest and breathing into her ruined mouth, but she was already gone.

When police arrived, they found a crime scene that differed significantly from the previous murders. This wasn't a random street attack or a robbery gone wrong. Someone had gained access to Sophia's home—someone she had trusted enough to let inside. Her shirt was pulled up and her bra undone, suggesting sexual assault had occurred before or after the murder.

The investigation into Sophia's death revealed troubling connections that would only make sense much later. Her phone records showed hundreds of calls to a number registered to a man named Mark Goudeau. The calls spanned most of 2005, suggesting an ongoing relationship between victim and killer.

But police investigating the murder had no reason to connect Mark Goudeau to the other Baseline killings. He was just another name in Sophia's contact list, another potential suspect to interview and eliminate. The connection would remain hidden until investigators finally identified the Baseline Killer and began piecing together the full scope of his crimes.

———

Carmen Miranda balanced her cell phone between her shoulder and ear as she fed quarters into the vacuum machine at the car wash on Thomas Road. Her boyfriend's voice crackled through the speaker as she began cleaning the interior of her vehicle, just another routine task on an ordinary evening.

"Hold on," she said, noticing someone approaching her car. "There's a guy—"

The boyfriend heard a male voice in the background: "Give me something."

Carmen's voice rose in alarm: "What? No, I don't have—"

Then the call went dead.

Security cameras captured what happened next. A man approached Carmen's vehicle and forced her into the backseat in what investigators would later call a "blitz attack." He then stole the car with Carmen inside, driving away into the Phoenix night.

Two hours later, police found the car abandoned in a secluded parking lot. Carmen's body was in the back seat, shot in the head and left in a degrading position with her pants partially pulled down. The killer had sexually assaulted her before the execution.

The brazen nature of the attack—occurring at a well-lit, public location with security cameras rolling—demonstrated the killer's complete lack of fear. He was hunting in broad daylight now, confident that he could take anyone, anywhere, at any time.

————

The DNA samples from the September attack on the two sisters had been sitting in the Phoenix police lab for months. Initial analysis suggested the samples were too degraded to yield useful results, so they were set aside while technicians focused on more promising evidence from other cases.

In early August 2006, the untested samples were sent to the Arizona State Laboratory, where analyst Lorraine Heath had access to more advanced equipment and newer testing procedures. She utilized a technique that could detect DNA from only the male chromosome, potentially yielding results from previously unusable evidence.

Heath worked methodically through the backlog, running each sample through multiple tests to extract every possible bit of genetic information. On September 2, she made the call that would change everything.

"I've got a hit," she told the Phoenix detective on the other end of the line. "The DNA from your sexual assault case matches someone in the database."

The name was Mark Goudeau, a forty-two-year-old ex-convict living in Phoenix. His DNA profile had been entered into the national database when he was released from prison on parole in 2004.

For the first time in over a year, investigators had a name to go with their killer.

———

Detective Alex Femenia stared at the photograph of Mark Goudeau that had been pulled from prison records. The face matched the composite sketch that had been plastered on billboards across Phoenix—light-skinned African American male, early forties, average build.

Mark Goudeau

Goudeau lived near 28th Street and Pinchot Avenue, just a few miles from several of the attack sites. He worked in construction and had been on parole since 2004, which explained why his DNA was in the system. His criminal history included aggravated assault and armed robbery, both involving violence against women.

As detectives began cross-referencing Goudeau's information with their case files, a disturbing connection emerged. Phone records from the Sophia Nunez murder showed over three hundred calls between her number and Goudeau's throughout 2005. They had known each other socially— neighbors or acquaintances who spoke regularly. The realization sent chills through the investigation team: The killer wasn't just hunting strangers. He was also targeting people who trusted him.

But having a suspect and proving a case were two different things. The DNA evidence connected Goudeau to one sexual assault, not to the string of murders that had terrorized Phoenix. Femenia needed more evidence—physical proof that would link this man to the other crimes.

On September 4, 2006, Phoenix police moved carefully. They arrested Goudeau in connection with the September 2005 sexual assault of the two sisters, a charge they could prove definitively through DNA evidence. However, they said nothing about the murder cases, letting him believe he was facing charges for a single sex crime.

Two days later, on Goudeau's forty-second birthday, detectives obtained a warrant to search his home. What they found there would seal the killer's fate and finally bring justice to the families of his victims.

———

The search of Goudeau's house began at dawn, with teams of investigators carefully cataloging every item that might connect him to the Baseline killings.

In the master bedroom, they found a pair of Nike sneakers that appeared to have been washed recently. Preliminary field tests detected traces of blood on the rubber soles, despite obvious attempts to clean them. The shoes were bagged as evidence and sent to the lab for DNA analysis.

A black ski mask hidden in a dresser drawer also tested positive for blood. Like the shoes, it showed signs of being laundered, but microscopic traces of biological evidence remained embedded in the fabric.

But the most damning evidence was found in the bedroom closet, hidden inside a Ziplock bag tucked into one of Goudeau's shoes. Detective Femenia opened the bag and found a gold ring with an inscription that made his blood run cold: "We love Mom." It was Tina Washington's ring, stolen from her body after the December murder.

The killer had kept it as a trophy—a memento of his kill. The discovery confirmed what investigators had suspected: They weren't dealing with someone who killed out of necessity or desperation. This was a predator who enjoyed his work enough to collect souvenirs.

Laboratory analysis of the shoes revealed blood from two murder victims: Chao Chou on the sole and Kristin Gibbons on the laces. The ski mask contained traces of Kristin's blood as well, suggesting Goudeau had worn it during her murder to avoid leaving DNA evidence at the scene.

The physical evidence was overwhelming. DNA samples tied Goudeau to multiple sexual assaults. Blood evidence linked him directly to specific murder victims. The stolen ring connected him to Tina Washington's killing. Most importantly, ballistics analysis confirmed that all nine murders had been committed with the same .380 caliber handgun—a weapon that was never recovered but had clearly been in Goudeau's possession.

———

As investigators dug deeper into Goudeau's background, a disturbing pattern emerged that stretched back decades.

In 1989, seventeen years before the Baseline killings, Goudeau had brutally attacked a woman named Darlene. He'd beaten her head with a barbell and attempted to drown her—an assault so vicious that she'd barely survived. Originally charged with sexual assault, kidnapping, and attempted murder, he'd had the rape charge dropped for lack of physical evidence and been convicted of aggravated assault. The following year, while awaiting sentencing, he'd attacked another woman with a shotgun and attempted to drown her as well, then committed an armed robbery at a Fry's supermarket.

The sentence was twenty-one years, but Goudeau had served only thirteen before being released on parole in 2004. Prison officials described him as a model inmate who had participated in rehabilitation programs and shown genuine remorse for his crimes. They believed he had been successfully reformed.

They were catastrophically wrong.

Within one year of his release, Goudeau had begun the killing spree that would claim nine lives and terrorize an entire city. The man who had convinced a parole board of his rehabilitation was actually a predator who had spent thirteen years learning how to be more careful, more methodical, and more deadly.

Those who knew Goudeau during his crime spree described him as friendly and normal. He was married to Wendy Carr, whom he had met through a prison pen-pal program. He worked in construction and maintained steady employment. Neighbors saw him as quiet and polite. Someone who kept to himself but caused no trouble.

The dichotomy was chilling. By day, Mark Goudeau was a reformed ex-convict trying to rebuild his life. By night, he was the Baseline Killer, hunting victims with a silver handgun.

———

The trial of Mark Goudeau became one of the most closely watched criminal proceedings in Arizona history. In 2007, he was convicted of nineteen felonies related to the sexual assault of the two sisters and sentenced to 438 years in prison. However, the murder charges still awaited their day in court.

In 2011, Goudeau faced a jury on seventy-four additional charges, including nine counts of first-degree murder. The trial was a massive undertaking, with prosecutors presenting the case in thirteen chronological chapters to help jurors understand the scope and progression of the killing spree.

Seven survivors testified against their attacker, identifying Goudeau as the man who had terrorized them. Peter Ochoa described seeing him standing over Tina Washington's body with a gun in his hand. The young son of Sophia Nunez, now a teenager, recounted finding his mother's body and trying desperately to save her life.

The evidence was crushing in its totality. DNA analysis, ballistics matching, eyewitness testimony, physical evidence, cell phone records, and the recovered trophies all pointed to the same inescapable conclusion: Mark Goudeau was the Baseline Killer.

On October 31, 2011, the jury found Goudeau guilty on sixty-seven of seventy-two counts, including all nine murder charges. A month later, he was sentenced to death nine times —once for each life he had taken—plus over a thousand years in prison for his other crimes.

————

The arrest and conviction of Mark Goudeau marked the end of one of the most terrifying periods in Phoenix history. For ten months, the city had lived under the shadow of a predator who could strike anywhere, anytime, without warning or mercy.

As of 2025, Mark Goudeau remains on death row at Arizona State Prison Complex, his appeals slowly working their way through the courts. The families of his nine murder victims continue to wait for final justice, while the survivors he left behind have had to rebuild their lives in the shadow of unimaginable trauma.

The teenagers who survived that first attack behind the church in August 2005 could never have imagined they were encountering one of Arizona's most notorious serial killers.

CHAPTER 12
THE CROWN HILL MURDER

L uke sent the text message at 11:21 a.m., but nobody would read it.

Luke Oberhansli stared at his phone screen, wondering why his girlfriend hadn't responded. His message was simple enough—just checking in, like he did every morning. Becky usually texted back within minutes, especially when she was home alone. She'd sent him "GOODIE XXXX" with heart emojis just twenty minutes earlier, her typical cheerful response when they made plans.

But now, nothing.

He tried calling. The phone rang and rang before going to voicemail. Luke frowned. Maybe she was in the shower. Maybe her phone had died. There were a dozen innocent explanations, and he cycled through them all as the morning stretched into afternoon. By evening, a cold knot had formed in his stomach. Something was wrong.

In the St George neighborhood of Bristol, sixteen-year-old Becky Watts had been looking forward to a quiet Thursday at home. February 19, 2015, was supposed to be an ordinary day. Her stepmother, Anjie Galsworthy, had left for a hospital appointment around eleven that morning, kissing Becky goodbye and telling her to text if she needed anything. Her father, Darren Galsworthy, was at work, dealing with the usual Thursday routine.

The house on Crown Hill stood silent.

————

Becky had come so far in recent months. After years of struggling with social anxiety so severe she'd sometimes come home from school in tears, unable to understand why she couldn't connect with her peers, she'd started to find her footing. The boxing lessons at her father's suggestion—unusual for someone so petite and quiet—had given her unexpected confidence. She was even mentoring younger students at the education center where she was resitting her GCSEs.

The Galsworthy household had its own unique rhythms. Darren had raised Becky and her brother, Danny, alone for years after gaining custody in 2002. When he married Anjie in April 2014, their families had merged into what appeared to be one cohesive unit. Anjie, despite her struggles with multiple sclerosis, had become more than a stepmother to Becky; she'd become her best friend and confidante, the one person who truly understood the girl's anxieties and fears.

Anjie's son, Nathan Matthews, had been part of Becky's life since she was a toddler. Her first word as a baby had been "Nathan," a fact that the family often recalled with fondness. At twenty-eight, Nathan lived across town with his girl-friend, Shauna Hoare, in a housing association house on Cotton Mill Lane. He worked as a delivery driver after failing to complete his electrician training—though he'd retained enough knowledge from his brief time in the military reserves to understand certain things about contamination and cleaning procedures. To the outside world, Nathan was just Anjie's son, the young man who'd served as best man at his mother's wedding to Darren less than a year earlier.

That Thursday morning, Nathan and Shauna had gone shopping at Tesco. They needed batteries, Nathan had said, though he didn't mention what for. After leaving, they'd driven to the Crown Hill home. Nathan had keys to his mother's house—of course he did. He was family. He was trusted.

———

When Anjie returned from her hospital appointment that evening at around 4:00 p.m., something felt immediately wrong. The house was too quiet. Becky's coat was gone—strange for a girl who rarely ventured out alone. Her bedroom door stood closed, and when Anjie pushed it open, the room was empty. The bed was made, and everything was in its place, but Becky wasn't there.

When Anjie called for Becky, her voice echoed through the empty house. No answer.

When Darren arrived home from work, he found Anjie in tears. Where was Becky? She wasn't answering her phone. Her boyfriend, Luke, had been trying to reach her all day, growing increasingly frantic with each unanswered call.

"Maybe she went to the library," Darren suggested weakly. But even as the words left his mouth, he knew they weren't true. Becky didn't just disappear. She needed routine, familiarity. The security of home.

Nathan and Shauna had been at the house earlier, Anjie mentioned through her tears. They'd stopped by while she was at her appointment. When Darren called Nathan, his stepson's voice sounded oddly flat.

"Yeah, we were there for a bit," Nathan said. "Left around noon. Becky was fine, just in her room doing her own thing."

"Did you talk to her?"

"Not really," he said, "You know how she is."

———

The hours that followed were torture. Darren walked the darkening streets of the St George neighborhood, checking every shop, every corner where his daughter might have gone. The park where she sometimes sat to think. The community center. Nothing. As night fell over Bristol, fear had completely replaced concern.

By Friday morning, with still no word from Becky and her phone going straight to voicemail, Darren couldn't wait any longer. At 4:00 p.m. on February 20—twenty-eight hours after anyone had last heard from his daughter—he walked into the Trinity Road Police Station. His hands trembled as he filled out the missing person report.

Detective Constable Liz Bees studied the man before her. A father barely holding himself together. His daughter, sixteen years old, history of anxiety, no previous instances of running away. When Bees asked for a recent photo, Darren's composure finally cracked as he handed over a picture from Becky's sixteenth birthday, just months earlier. She was smiling, a rare moment of pure happiness captured forever.

The machinery of a missing person investigation began its relentless turn. Officers arrived at the Crown Hill house as darkness fell on Friday night. They needed more photos, a list of friends, and any place Becky might go. The family gathered in the living room—Darren, Anjie, and Danny. Nathan arrived soon after, having heard the news from his mother.

"She wouldn't just leave," Anjie kept repeating, rocking back and forth on the sofa. "Something's happened to her. I know it."

Nathan sat beside his mother, arm around her shoulders. "She's probably just needed some space," he said. "You know how teenagers are."

Detective Sergeant John Dowding watched the family dynamics carefully. In his experience, the first hours of a missing person case revealed everything or nothing. His priority was Becky's digital footprint—teenagers lived their lives online. If she'd run away, there would be signs.

But the technical team's report was troubling. Becky's phone had gone completely silent at 11:21 a.m. on Thursday. Her last text to Luke, then nothing. No calls, no messages, no social media updates. The phone's last known location was the Crown Hill house.

As Friday night bled into Saturday morning, search teams spread out across the St George neighborhood of Bristol. Officers knocked on doors in the freezing February darkness, showing Becky's photo to bleary-eyed residents. They checked her usual haunts—the education center where she studied, the boxing gym she'd recently joined—but found nothing. It was as if Becky Watts had simply vanished.

Nathan and Shauna remained at the family home through the night, making tea and offering comfort, but something about them struck the family liaison officers as off. When DS Dowding asked them to come to the station to give formal witness statements—standard procedure for anyone who'd been at the house that day—they exchanged a look.

"Is that really necessary?" Nathan asked. "We've told you everything. We left before anything happened."

"It's just routine," Dowding assured them. "You might have seen something you didn't realize was important."

Shauna, who had barely spoken all evening, seemed to shrink into herself. Nathan's jaw tightened, but he nodded. "Tomorrow, then. We'll come tomorrow."

They didn't come tomorrow.

By Saturday, February 21, the search had exploded into a major operation. Detective Chief Inspector Richard Ocone had taken command of what was rapidly becoming one of the largest missing person investigations in Avon and Somerset Police history. The media had seized the story—a vulnerable teenager vanishing from her own home. The family's desperate plea for information led every local newscast.

Behind the scenes, something was troubling DCI Ocone. As part of standard procedure, police had taken DNA samples and fingerprints from all family members and close contacts; they needed to eliminate them from any evidence found at the scene. It was routine, explained as a way to identify Becky's belongings if found. Nathan had seemed reluctant but had complied. Shauna's hands had been shaking so badly she could barely press her fingers to the scanner.

The search expanded through the weekend. Volunteers joined police in combing through St George Park, Troopers Hill nature reserve, and the woods at Oldbury Court. The hashtag #FindBecky spread across social media like wildfire. Becky's school photo—that shy smile, those vulnerable eyes —was shared thousands of times.

On Monday, February 23, Darren and Becky's grandmother, Pat, faced the media at a press conference. The room was packed with journalists and cameras, pressing in with the weight of public attention. Darren could barely speak through his tears.

"Becky, if you're watching this, please come home," he managed. "You're not in trouble. We just want you back. We love you so much."

Behind him, Nathan stood with the rest of the family, his face a mask of concern. When a reporter asked if the family had any idea where Becky might have gone, Nathan stepped forward.

"She's been struggling lately," he said, his voice steady. "With anxiety and stuff. But she's strong. We just want her home safe."

The words sounded right, but something in his delivery made DCI Ocone's instincts prickle. He'd been doing this job for fifteen years, and something about Nathan Matthews didn't sit right.

On February 24, five days into the search, crime scene investigators returned to the Crown Hill house for a more detailed examination. CSI Claire Dymond worked methodically through each room with ultraviolet lights and chemical reagents. In Becky's bedroom, those small stains on the door frame that Anjie had noticed glowed under her equipment.

Blood. Multiple spots of blood.

Dymond photographed everything, then took samples for DNA analysis. The lab was told to fast-track the results. This was no longer looking like a simple runaway.

The blood was Becky's. But there was something else— something that made DCI Ocone's blood run cold when he received the call on February 27. On one of the bloodstains, high on the door frame, forensic scientists had found a fingerprint preserved in the blood itself. The print was perfect, every ridge and whorl captured in Becky's blood like a signature.

They ran it through the database of elimination prints they'd collected from the family.

It matched Nathan Matthews.

DCI Ocone sat alone in his office, staring at the report. Nathan's print in Becky's blood meant he'd touched that spot during or immediately after she'd been injured.

But Nathan had told them repeatedly that he'd left the house before anything had happened to Becky. That he'd barely seen her that day.

———

The decision to bring Nathan and Shauna in had to be handled delicately. They couldn't flee—police had been discreetly monitoring them for days. On February 28, nine days after Becky's disappearance, two police cars pulled up outside the Cotton Mill Lane address.

Nathan Matthews and Shauna Hoare

Nathan answered the door, and his face went pale when he saw DCI Ocone.

"Is this about Becky? Have you found her?"

"We need you and Shauna to come to the station," Ocone said evenly. "There are some questions we need to ask."

"We've already told you everything."

"Please, Nathan. It's important."

In the back of one of the cars, Shauna was crying silently, tears streaming down her face. Nathan stared straight ahead, his hands clenched into fists.

At the Kenneth Steele House police station, they were placed in separate interview rooms. DCI Ocone decided to begin with Shauna, hoping she might break without Nathan present.

She sat rigidly in the plastic chair, arms wrapped around herself. The duty solicitor beside her had to repeatedly remind her to speak up for the recording. Her story came out in fragments. They'd gone to check on the house. Nathan had wanted to tidy up for his mother. They'd left around noon. Becky was in her room.

"Did Nathan go into Becky's room?"

Shauna's eyes darted to the door, as if Nathan might burst through it. "I... I don't know. Maybe."

"Shauna, this is very important. Did you see Nathan go into Becky's room?"

A long silence. Then, barely audible: "He told me to wait downstairs."

In the adjacent interview room, Nathan was maintaining his story with aggressive insistence. He claimed they'd been there briefly and left before anything had happened, but he hadn't been in Becky's room. When DCI Ocone placed the forensic report on the table—Nathan's finger-print in Becky's blood—Nathan's lawyer requested a break.

When they resumed, Nathan's demeanor had changed. Gone was the cooperation, replaced by sullen silence.

"I want to go home," he said.

"Nathan, your fingerprint was in your stepsister's blood. She's missing. You need to tell us what happened."

"No comment."

They couldn't hold them without charging them, not yet. However, when Nathan and Shauna were released that evening, a search team was already at their Cotton Mill Lane home with a warrant.

What CSI Dymond found in their bathroom made her step back and call for additional support.

The bathroom had been cleaned with an intensity that bordered on obsession. The smell of bleach was overwhelming, burning the investigators' eyes, but bleach couldn't hide everything. In the grout between tiles, in the microscopic imperfections of the ceramic, traces remained.

When the lights were turned off and luminol was applied, the bathroom transformed into a constellation of horror. Blue luminescence revealed blood everywhere—the walls, the floor, the bathtub itself. Someone had tried desperately to clean up a massive amount of blood.

On March 2, Nathan Matthews and Shauna Hoare were arrested on suspicion of murder. This time, there would be no release.

The questioning was relentless. DCI Ocone laid out the evidence methodically. The fingerprint. The blood in their bathroom. CCTV footage they'd uncovered from February 20—the day after Becky's disappearance—showing Nathan at B&Q purchasing a circular saw. An £80 MacAllister 1400-watt circular saw, to be precise.

Nathan's solicitor requested break after break, hushed conversations with his client growing more urgent. Shauna, in her interview room, had stopped responding entirely, sitting in catatonic silence.

———

On the morning of March 3, Nathan's solicitor informed detectives that his client wished to make a statement.

Nathan sat across from DCI Ocone, his face gray and eyes hollow. For a long moment, nobody spoke. The tape recorder hummed. Then Nathan began.

"There was an accident. Becky's dead."

Even though Ocone had suspected this outcome, hearing the words was like a physical blow. He kept his expression neutral, professional.

"Tell me what happened, Nathan."

The story Nathan told was this: He and Shauna had gone to the house to talk to Becky about her behavior, about how she treated his mother. There had been an argument. Becky had attacked him, and in the struggle to restrain her, she'd stopped breathing. He claimed it was an accident and he'd panicked.

"Where is she now?"

Nathan provided an address: 9 Barton Court. A shed in the back garden, less than a hundred meters from his own home.

The convoy that arrived at Barton Court moved with grim efficiency. The property belonged to Karl Demetrius, who stood in his doorway, bewildered, claiming to know nothing. Nathan had asked to store some belongings, he said. Just some boxes.

Inside the shed, investigators found black suitcases, bags, and boxes wrapped in meters and meters of cling film. The smell hit them first—decomposition mixed with salt and cat litter. An attempt to mask the unmistakable odor of death.

What they discovered inside those packages would haunt even the most experienced officers. Becky hadn't just been killed. Her body had been systematically dismembered—cut into eight pieces with the circular saw Nathan had purchased. Each part was wrapped with meticulous care, packaged with a precision that spoke to planning, to careful thought about concealment.

The investigation exploded with new evidence. Nathan's computer revealed searches for body disposal methods, for power tools capable of cutting through bone. Text messages between Nathan and Shauna contained discussions about kidnapping "schoolgirls," about teaching someone a lesson.

In the Cotton Mill Lane house, hidden in a cupboard, police found two stun guns capable of delivering 8,000 volts, along with handcuffs, masks, and tape. This wasn't the equipment of someone planning a conversation. This was a kidnap kit.

Investigators discovered CCTV footage from a Tesco store where they bought batteries to power the stun guns.

The truth that emerged was more horrific than anyone had imagined. Nathan had harbored a deep obsession with teenage girls, particularly "petite" ones. His computer contained over 270 images and twenty-one videos of violent pornography involving teenagers. One video, seventeen minutes long, showed a teenager being attacked in her own home.

On that Thursday morning, with the house empty, Nathan had attempted to kidnap his sixteen-year-old stepsister—but Becky had fought back. The forty separate injuries to her face told the story of a desperate struggle for life. In that struggle, Nathan had suffocated her.

After the murder, in an act of rage or twisted dominance, he had stabbed her fifteen times.

———

The trial began on October 6, 2015, at Bristol Crown Court. For six weeks, the jury heard evidence that made several members physically ill. The prosecution, led by

William Mousley QC, presented over 1,200 pieces of evidence.

Nathan maintained his story of an accident, claiming he'd only meant to scare Becky. The evidence told a different story. The kidnap kit. The violent pornography. The meticulous dismemberment and cover-up. The post-mortem stab wounds.

Despite Shauna's claims of complete ignorance, her DNA was on the masks found with Becky's remains, and her fingerprints covered the tape. She'd clearly been there, and she had participated.

The most devastating testimony came from Becky's family. They described how Nathan had comforted them during the search, had suggested places to look, and had held his mother while she cried—all while knowing exactly what he'd done.

On November 11, 2015, after just three hours of deliberation, the jury delivered its verdict. Nathan Matthews: guilty of murder. Shauna Hoare: guilty of manslaughter. Both guilty of conspiracy to kidnap, preventing lawful burial, and perverting the course of justice.

On November 13, Justice Dingemans delivered the sentences, his voice breaking with emotion. Nathan Matthews received life imprisonment with a minimum of thirty-three years. Shauna Hoare received seventeen years.

"You, Nathan Matthews, have been convicted of the murder of your sixteen-year-old stepsister," the judge said with tears building in his eyes. "The planned kidnap of Becky was for a sexual purpose. You had a fixation with having sex with petite teenage girls."

Becky's father, Darren, stood in the public gallery, supported by family members as the man he'd raised as a son was led away to begin a sentence that would keep him imprisoned until at least 2048.

In her victim impact statement, Becky's mother, Tanya, described seeing her daughter's mutilated body in the mortuary, an image that would haunt her forever. Darren spoke of how their entire world had collapsed when they'd learned the truth—that the danger hadn't come from outside, but from within their own family.

The Watts family had been destroyed by the ultimate betrayal. Becky, who had struggled with anxiety about the dangers of the outside world, had been murdered in her own home by someone she'd known since she was a baby. Someone whose name had been her first word.

As the prison van carried Nathan Matthews away from Bristol Crown Court, protesters lined the streets. Inside the vehicle, however, Nathan showed no emotion. The man who had killed his stepsister, dismembered her body, and then comforted her grieving parents simply stared straight ahead.

Shauna Hoare was paroled in September 2023, after serving only eight and a half years. She was banned from returning to Bristol. Nathan Matthews remains in prison, where he was reportedly attacked by other inmates who threw boiling butter at him. Even among criminals, some crimes are considered unforgivable.

Online Appendix

Visit my website for additional photos and videos pertaining to the cases in this book:

http://TrueCrimeCaseHistories.com/vol20/

More books by Jason Neal

Looking for more?? I am constantly adding new volumes of True Crime Case Histories. The series **can be read in any order**, and all books are available in paperback, hardcover, and audiobook.

Check out the complete series on Amazon series at:

https://geni.us/JasonNeal

FREE BONUS EBOOK FOR MY READERS

As my way of saying "Thank you" for reading, I'm giving away a FREE True Crime e-book I think you'll enjoy.

https://TrueCrimeCaseHistories.com

Just visit the link above to let me know where to send your free book!

THANK YOU!

Thank you for reading this Volume of True Crime Case Histories. I truly hope you enjoyed it. If you did, I would be sincerely grateful if you would take a few minutes to write a review for me on Amazon using the link below.

https://geni.us/TrueCrime20

I'd also like to encourage you to sign up for my email list for updates, discounts, and freebies on future books! I promise I'll make it worth your while with future freebies.

http://truecrimecasehistories.com

And please take a moment and follow me on Amazon.

http://amazon.com/author/jason-neal/

Thanks so much,

Jason Neal

ABOUT THE AUTHOR

Jason Neal is a Best-Selling American True Crime Author living in Hawaii with his Turkish-British wife. Jason started his writing career in the late eighties as a music industry publisher and wrote his first true crime collection in 2019.

As a boy growing up in the eighties just south of Seattle, Jason became interested in true crime stories after hearing the news of the Green River Killer so close to his home. Over the subsequent years, he would read everything he could get his hands on about true crime and serial killers.

As he approached 50, Jason began to assemble stories of the crimes that have fascinated him most throughout his life. He's especially obsessed by cases solved by sheer luck, amazing police work, and groundbreaking technology like early DNA cases and, more recently, reverse genealogy.

Printed in Dunstable, United Kingdom